MW00904329

Always Balanced *and* Connected

Daily Affirmations for Body, Mind and Spirit

Maggie Davis-Jelly, LCSW

Foreword by Dr. Charlie McNeil

Contributors:
Dr. Dana G. Cohen and Jill Rodda, MS

Balboa Press books may be ordered through booksellers or by contacting:

Balboa Press
A Division of Hay House
1663 Liberty Drive
Bloomington, IN 47403
www.balboapress.com
1 (877) 407-4847

Print information available on the last page.

ISBN: 978-1-5043-3580-5 (sc)
ISBN: 978-1-5043-3582-9 (hc)
ISBN: 978-1-5043-3581-2 (e)

Library of Congress Control Number: 2015910501

Balboa Press rev. date: 10/23/2015

What People Are Saying

What a wonderful book for everyone. Maggie helps us to connect with, and live our lives from, our souls. The challenge of breaking through the shell of past hurts and negative ideas that separate each of us from a deeply loving and joyful experience of ourselves and life is well addressed in Maggie's work.

The format is inspiring. In each short section, Maggie presents an affirmation that flows into an intention. She then follows with a thoughtful elaboration, nicely expanding each concept in a self-illuminating fashion. This invites one to spend a few moments of meditation on the idea, expanding one's own thoughts about it and applying it to one's life. Affirmations and intentions presented in this way are naturally carried into the rest of our day, operating in the background of our mind. They continue to have a positive effect, whether one goes on to think consciously about it or gets caught up in the routine of the day.

This is one of those books wherein one can employ synchronicity and ask, "What does the universe have to send me today?" and then open to any page, and read.

We live in an age where we are so easily pulled off course in our search for existential meaning. By being mindful, in the here and now, our greatest experience of life is attained when we are able to bask in the ember of the moment, and Maggie's work helps us find the joy and love that only being in the now can bring.

I am very grateful to have the opportunity to benefit from Maggie's collection of inspirations and applications, which are written in such a thoughtful way. This is a beautiful work.

—Pierce Skinner, PsyD, Green Village, NJ

Always Balanced and Connected: Daily Affirmations for Body, Mind and Spirit is for those of you caught up in the balancing act of life, everyone! The art of living is being able to take what comes your way, while enjoying and maintaining health and wellness. A task much easier said than done, however possible. Daily reflections serve to guide you through each day. Perhaps something will resonate with your life experiences. Poets, philosophers, athletes, saints and sinners give words of inspiration, encouragement and answers to the question, "Why?" The questions and answers of the past create incentive for the future. "Always Balanced and Connected: Daily Affirmations for Body, Mind and Spirit" provides you with the tools necessary for a healthy lifestyle and possibly the answer to your question, "Why?"

—Devin O'Brien, Rutgers University, New Jersey

Maggie's new book provides affirmations that are quite congruent with many of today's challenges. Self-actuating and appropriate for all. With a focus on mindfulness these affirmations are especially well suited for use in conjunction with the twelve step program, but also appropriate for other self help, DBT and many of today's therapeutic approaches. A refreshing and contemporary addition to the affirmation books we already use at our facilities.

—Nelson L. Hadler, MSW, LCSW, LCADC, CCS, Executive Director, Treatment Dynamics of Summit, New Jersey

Hoping I live at least most of my life by Maggie's affirmations!

—Lt. Col. Gary W. Trageser, USAF (ret)

Maggie is an amazing psychotherapist, dedicated to helping families. I have referred many divorce clients to her and I have always received positive feedback.

—Faith A. Ullman, Esq., Newton, New Jersey

The affirmations are uplifting!

—Dawn Marie Hamilton, author of *Sea Panther*

Happiness is a dynamic state that requires effort to achieve and sustain. One must demand their happiness from themselves, and being intentional about that process is critical. The lack of proper tools is a common barrier to progress, but "Always Balanced and Connected: Daily Affirmations for Body, Mind, and Spirit" is an instrument that one can consistently turn to amidst the tumult of their life.

—Michael May, Boston, Massachusetts

Daily Affirmations are words to live by for a true and meaningful life. They are a gift I give myself each morning to feed my spirit and help it grow. The "how to" steps included help with the practical application of these universal principles. The daily readings are a small investment in time, yielding BIG results! Thank you Maggie Jelly for daily devotions, which bring peace to the mind, body and spirit.

—Donna Centrelli, Spiritual Guide

It is a book I would keep next to me in my bedroom and read everyday. I feel so inspired I'm going to take a yoga class this afternoon!

—Kelly Pampin, BSW, Ramapo College of New Jersey

Wow-what a project-one that is especially needed in this world gone awry of personal responsibility and basic ethics.

—Dr. Michele Takacs, Lafayette, New Jersey

I thoroughly enjoyed it. I have nothing but praise for Always Balanced and Connected: Daily Affirmations for Body, Mind and Spirit. It's a great book! Maggie Davis--Jelly writes with the well being of others in mind.

—Marie Grace O'Brien, deacon's wife, St. Kateri Tekawitha RC Church, Sparta, New Jersey

I loved it! ... Maggie obviously put a lot of heart and soul into it. I'll share it with my clients.

—Dr. Seth Ersner-Hersfeld, Psychological Associates, Sussex County, New Jersey

This is a true labor of love; that message shines through. There is so much good stuff in here! Of all the affirmations, my favorites are the ones on perfection (how not to be!) faith, worrying, and sunsets! Teens would also benefit greatly from the wisdom in these pages.

—Maryann McFadden, author of *The Book Lover*, *So Happy Together*, and *The Richest Season*

In this day and age of electronic relationships and fast paced work and even social schedules, it is even more important to take a moment each day to affirm the true nature of why we are here. In this book Maggie does just that by giving us concrete examples and affirmations. I find them to be thoughtful and inspiring!

—Arlene Michel Rich, The Spiritual Awakening

What a wonderful concept with a positive message for all. The daily affirmations truly give you an opportunity to step back from the daily grind and reconnect with your better self. I will be making this a daily ritual.

—Trevor O'Brien, Harvard University,
Boston, Massachusetts

Service to others is healing and creates new and strong vibrations to those who give of themselves. Maggie has always been willing to assist Hands On the World Global in the years we have been helping those in developing nations. Maggie's contribution has helped to increase the team effort of vibration allowing others to follow.

—Rachael Paulson, founder HOWGlobal.org

The book is terrific - very uplifting and inspirational. What a wonderful gift for your patients and anyone else who reads it. Faith, prayer and meditation are the best alternative medicines!

—Deborah Templeton, APNC, Lac

Maggie has captured the essence of reflection through quotes and ideas and turned them into a connection of everyday life. Truly thought provoking.

—Donna Fell, Sparta, NJ

In Memoriam

In loving memory of my mother
Agnes Mae Davis
"A"
an original "Rosie the Riveter"
1916–2015.

And in memory of my friend Julie Garforth, 1957–2011.

Dedicated to

My husband Bill, who has taught me
patience, kindness and mutual understanding.
To Evan for teaching me to be a better person,
Alex for teaching me strength and generosity, and
Nora for teaching me how to care and to listen.
Their love is the source of my strength and inspiration.

To Mitch Kahn, LCSW, of Ramapo College of New Jersey (ret) Whenever I was puzzled or not completely certain what to do, I thought to myself, *what would Mitch do?* The best thing about knowing Mitch is how fun it is to just sit back and watch him get things done. Mitch is a humble man. I am not quite certain he is aware of the multitude of people he has influenced in a major way. I have never met a student—past or present—or anyone else, for that matter, who did not have amazingly glowing things to say about Mitch. Mitch is a *true social worker with a heart, conscience, and purpose.* Hey, Mitch, you rock!

Dreams, Goals, and Affirmations

The idea for this book is simple. I wanted something that could be made available to people that incorporates the reason that a connection of oneness is vital to health and wellness. Additionally, my intention with *Always Balanced and Connected: Daily Affirmations for Body, Mind, and Spirit* is to create an educational component for mental health workers, therapists, doctors, nurses, counselors, clergy, and all professionals working in the medical/behavioral health field that will illuminate the body–mind–spirit connection. I have been blogging for quite some time on Facebook as "Daily Affirmations for Body, Mind, and Soul" and have been well received by audiences from around the world. I would like to share my concept with you. I believe in miracles, and together we can make them happen.

—Maggie

Foreword

The Body, Mind and Spirit Connection

Medical scientists, physicians and the overall health and wellness professional community dedicate their lives to educate, develop and improve upon the efficacy of the "Mind-Body" connection. Who of us is not familiar with tension headaches, tight shoulder, neck, and back muscles from too much perceived stress? Or butterflies in the stomach before a speaking engagement? Or blushing when embarrassed? Or breaking out in a sweat when anxious? Or even to the point of a full-blown heart pounding, breath taking, sweating palms, and light-headedness of a panic attack? Conversely, we are also aware of how practices such as meditation, prayer, and yoga can relax our bodies, which in turn can calm our minds and soothe our spirits for more efficient and healthy functioning while bringing about a sense of wellness and wholeness of our entire being.

Perhaps the "Mind-Spirit" connection is not quite as popular a concept. We use the words *"mind"* and *"spirit"* all the time and there is a certain common understanding that people share in every day speech. Consider how we use the word *mind*: "Do you mind if I go early?" "We are all of one mind here." "Mind your manners." "Are you changing your mind again?" The use of the word *spirit* is equally common: "She has a sweet spirit." "Following the winning season, the school spirit is at an all-time high." "That contestant has a lot of spirit." "I need something to lift my spirit." There are many different contexts and nuances for each term.

When we try to put a specific definition to the words, however, it becomes apparent that their explanations can be fuzzy, vague, imprecise, or sometimes even contradictory, depending on who may be speaking, what their understanding is, and how the words are being used. For clarity, let's go back to some baseline, original terms. Another older word for "*mind*" is "*psyche*"—the same root which forms the word *psychology,* or the study of the mind. In this context, the "mind" consists of the conscious and unconscious mental functions related to our personality: how and what we think, how and what we perceive, how and what we feel, the way we reason, as well as what constitutes our will and the choices we make, our memory, and our imagination. More poetically, it involves everything that is processed in and through both our head and our heart.

"Spirit" refers to the vital, dynamic force of being—what makes us alive, sentient beings and distinguishes us from inanimate objects that are not living. Ancient words related to *spirit* include the Hebrew *ruach* (breath, an invisible force or power), the Greek *pneuma* (breath, wind), the Latin *spiritus* (spirit, breath), and the Sanskrit *prana* (a life breath or vital principle). Spirituality involves becoming more focused on the essential experience of being deeply, fully alive and cultivating an awareness of and connection to a greater Life Force (whether this is identified as God, Spirit, Self, Universe, or by any other name). Religions are more formalized organizations with structures, beliefs, understandings, and consequent moral and ethical codes based on the spiritual experience of the religion's founder(s). *Spirit* does not consist of specific beliefs, but is more of an experience. A wise teacher was counseling someone who did not believe she was very "spiritual." Rather than getting bogged down with religious understandings, beliefs, or dogmas (which the person was assuming was "spiritual"), the teacher simply asked, "What makes you feel most alive? When you feel most alive is when you are most connected to your spirit!"

One way of understanding how the two are connected is to refer to our core, living, being, spirit-"Self" (capital "S") which energizes and enlivens our thoughts-feelings-personality mind-"self" (small "s"). In one sense we don't have as much direct access to the spirit-Self, but we can give attention, use our imagination, and create thoughts with our mind-self that can connect with the spirit-Self. This is the whole idea behind spiritual exercises, whether they be reading and contemplation of sacred writings, prayer, meditation, journaling, meditation, yoga, etc. The more willing, open, and receptive we are to cultivating the connection, the more whole we become.

One of the difficulties that cause interference in the connection between mind-self and spirit-Self is what some have called "monkey mind." This is what we notice when we try to sit down and quiet our minds and contrary to our intention, our "monkey minds" chatter and screech and jump from limb to limb and keep active with all kinds of thoughts, feelings, perceptions, imaginations, etc. This can be overcome by paying attention to our breathing and doing a simple meditation exercise of re-focusing on our breathing over and over. We can start to tame the wild monkeys (refocus on the breathing... and again... and again!) that want to keep introducing every kind of distraction possible to divert, entertain, confuse, and sidetrack us! Others who find meditation too difficult might do better with a contemplation exercises of reading something inspiring, positive, and uplifting; mulling over the thoughts and ideas presented; and letting them "sink in." This is enhanced with following up and writing down some insights in a journal. Writing is a particularly helpful practice because thoughts and ideas that may be floating around in our heads take on a more tangible reality when written down. This can be a clarification process, where the written word provides more precision and illumination, we tend to "own" it more, plus a written record is easier to return to and notice changes in thoughts, understandings, and awareness over focus our time.

Another difficulty is the clutter of our mind-self that clogs the connection to spirit-Self, such as the self-defeating, habitual stressful thoughts and feelings like anger, sadness, negativity, jealousy, greed, impatience, etc. If these are very strong and intrusive in your life, it may be helpful to get some assistance from a sensitive pastor, priest, rabbi, imam, or therapist.

In addition to meditation and contemplation, mantras or short statements such as affirmations can be very helpful in moving from mind-self to spirit-Self. Wisdom of the ancients informs us, "As we think in our hearts, so we are." What we focus on has a way of shaping our thoughts, which influences our feelings, and can create more positive, productive actions and behaviors. If we think negative thoughts, anticipate bad outcomes, or dwell on what is or could be wrong, that kind of focus expands and fills our consciousness and ultimately starts to impact our physical health adversely, as well. On the other hand, as we think positive thoughts, anticipate productive outcomes, and focus on what is good, a whole different context is created. Other ancient insight directs us: "whatever is true, whatever is honorable, whatever is just, whatever is pure, whatever is pleasing, whatever is commendable, if there is any excellence and if there is anything worthy of praise, think about these things." That wisdom and spiritual truth is the bedrock foundation of this book, "Always Balanced and Connected: Daily Affirmations for Body, Mind, and Spirit."

An advantage of affirmations is that they are portable. You can copy an affirmation on a card and carry it with you, refer to it throughout the day at a stoplight, while taking a bathroom break, before starting a new task, etc., and let it marinate in your mind as new neural pathways in your brain are created, deeper connections to your spirit are enhanced, and a greater sense of well-being is achieved integrating your body, mind, and spirit into a healthier whole.

-Dr. Charlie McNeil, L.M.F.T.

Leading You Toward a Healthier Future

According to the Consortium of Academic Health Centers for Integrative Medicine, integrative medicine is "the practice of medicine that reaffirms the importance of the relationship between practitioner and patient, focuses on the whole person, is informed by evidence, and makes use of all appropriate therapeutic approaches, health-care professionals and disciplines to achieve optimal health and healing."

Medicine is an art. A patient-centered, holistic approach can lead to the path to overall health and wellness. A wide variety of treatments, services and dietary recommendations can help to fill the gaps in cases where traditional medicine has reached its limit, and can help enhance the benefits of traditional medicine by considering a patient's whole lifestyle when determining the best course of action.

The uniqueness of each person's biochemical processes is only just beginning to be appreciated by traditional medicine. To illustrate, I feel that holistic medicine can provide great relief to those suffering from stress and anxiety. Stress producing anxiety should be treated if intense (more than people usually feel), chronic (felt many times during the day or most days of the week), or limiting (making it hard to do daily tasks or relate to others). Different forms of anxiety are linked to different chemical imbalances in the body. Levels of norepinephrine, dopamine, and serotonin, and many other chemicals can affect anxiety. Symptoms of anxiety may include fatigue, restlessness, poor concentration, excessive sweating, irritability, headaches, muscle tension, trembling, sleep problems, and elevated heart rate.

To further illustrate, nutritional counseling (an alternative approach to healing), can help you take control of your health by optimizing your diet. The food that we eat today hardly resembles the diet of our early ancestors. We evolved to digest and benefit from the food in our environment, and our body uses the nutrients, minerals, and proteins from what we ingest to grow, strengthen, and maintain its form. However, in some cases, because of the increase and availability of processed foods, many people are not getting the nutrients they need from their diet or, worse, are being harmed by the food they are eating. Calcium, iron, and vitamin deficiencies can often be remedied by few simple changes to your diet. Be your own best advocate in your quest for health and wellness. Be educated, be diligent, be balanced and be well.

— Dana G. Cohen, MD

Prologue

The Answers Are Within You

Self-awareness, authenticity, and a desire to be whole in body, mind, and spirit are essential to make the connection and live a purposeful and balanced life. Our bodies desperately try to give us warning signals and want us to be well. We have the ability to heal ourselves. *Always Balanced and Connected: Affirmations for Body, Mind, and Spirit* focuses on the basic concept of every day. Taking care of you first and prioritizing your health and wellness are essential to living a happy, healthy, and well-adjusted life. Be aware that *your* physical, mental, and spiritual health are priority one.

Familiarize yourself with yourself. Accept who you are. Be comfortable in your own skin, and know that you are amazing! Love yourself, and connect your capabilities with the possibilities you have before you. The possibilities are endless for you to succeed in life and love. Your dreams, passions, and desires are of your spirit. Allow them to manifest, flourish, and take flight. Affirm who you are, embrace your experiences and your beliefs, and understand your ability to adapt. Do not be afraid of change. Your faith will guide you. After all, life is merely a series of adjustments.

Nutrition, exercise, and rest lend support to the relationship you have with your body. They are integrated and dependent on each other. If only one of the three components is missing from your personal health plan, the quality of your health suffers. What is a personal health plan?

Developing and maintaining a personal health plan takes planning, consistency, and a positive attitude.

1) Make nutritious and delicious meal choices. Create a desire to be your best self, and reject negativity, criticism, and the fear of failure. Planning is vital. Plan ahead to eat healthy meals. Choose foods deliberately. Manage your eating habits. Overeating or making poor choices is simply a bad habit. Exchange a poor choice with a healthier version. We all slip up, and that's okay. Simply try again tomorrow. Reaffirm your goals. Having more than one doughnut is like wearing a wool sweater down south in July! Your body doesn't benefit from it. Plan your meals with a critical mind-set.
2) Develop an appropriate exercise plan to support your individual goals. Take a personal inventory of what you want to get out of your exercise routine. Whether it is doing yoga, walking, toning and strength training, running, or dancing, commit to at least four times a week for twenty minutes. To maintain your exercise plan, it must be enjoyable. Do what *you* like, or you will not do it for long. Friends are fine as exercise buddies, but only if their desire is compatible with yours and they want to achieve the same results. For some, social exercise is good, but for others it's not. Know yourself, and don't be afraid to do what works for you. Put yourself first, and be happy with your method of movement. Get yourself workout clothes, suitable to your activity, no matter your size. You will

look great, and it will give you the incentive to keep it up!

3) Take time to rest. Allowing time for recovery is essential for good hormones to facilitate restful sleep, weight loss, and endurance in your daily rounds. It also will contribute to a positive attitude. Get enough sleep at night—seven to eight hours is best. Try to wake up every morning at the same time, and go to sleep at the same time every night. Dr. Frank Kane of Skylands Medical Group in Newton, New Jersey, recommends taking a short, "10 Minute Cap Nap" during the day, every day if possible. Nothing is more important on your daily list of things to do.
4) Consistency is most important in maintaining good health. You need to teach your body to work properly by eating well, having a regular exercise program, and allowing enough rest. Your body will function better through muscle growth and an increase in good hormones. The combination of both of these things will fuel your metabolism and give you more energy and an overall feeling of being healthy and well.

You have to feel, and do the work, if you want to heal and be well!

—Maggie Davis-Jelly, LCSW and Jill Rodda, MS

-Please check with a health-care professional prior to beginning a new exercise routine or changing eating habits. This is general information only.

Introduction

When everything in your life is in place, you will find peace. Find peace and everything will fall into place.

I practice affirmations from a multitude of sources in my daily life. Poems, lyrics, and books all send a message for which I've been waiting. When I ask for help, help comes—not when I want it necessarily, but when I need it. A message might come in the form of a song on the radio or a sign on the road. My intention is that *Always Balanced and Connected: Daily Affirmations for Body, Mind, and Spirit* will be a guide to help you recognize your own needs and to determine what is or isn't working in your life. My hope is that it encourages you to look at your life in a different way, just for today.

The people in my life keep me balanced and connected—balanced in body, mind, and spirit, and connected to my work, my playful activities, my friends, my family, my community, and my solitude. The people in my life encourage me. When I am out of balance, not being my authentic self, not feeling well, and not on my game, something has to give.

When what I say and do is in alignment, all is well. When I am healthy physically and emotionally, I have the ability to react to situations in a positive way. My spirit takes flight! I experience grace, peace, and harmony. It's a tall order! It does happen, and my goal in life is to reach a point where joy outlives sorrow.

The concept of spirit and connectedness often needs clarification. The concept is confusing to many; spirituality, in my book, is not to be confused with religion. Simply put, spiritual connectedness, to me, means that we're not in this world alone, nor are we alone in our personal lives. Spirit is the breath of life. When we cease to breathe, we die.

I ask you to look at the concept of being balanced and connected in body, mind, and spirit in a new or perhaps slightly different light. Take a breath, and experience the goodness in your soul. I will use the word *God* from time to time, because it is used in quotations of some of the most influential thinkers of our time. God is spirit, animation, or energy. Similar words used to describe God are *energy*, *vigor*, *vitality*, *life*, and *spirit*. Please feel free to substitute your personal source of spirit for all that is good in your life as you read the following pages.

The Golden Rule, "Love thy neighbor as thyself," is universal. Mindful meditation is prayer. The only prayers you will ever need are "Please," "Thank you," "I need help," and "Thank you for the blessings of joy and love surrounding me."

Being physically healthy and maintaining overall health and wellness also can be extremely confusing to most of us in the Western world. Poisons and toxins are in the food we eat, the water we drink, and the air we breathe. Legal and illegal substances, not to mention a sedentary lifestyle and downright bad choices, lead to poor physical health, depression, and anxiety. Can you have a healthy body, mind, and spirit connection? Can you experience being the best you can be? Yes, you can! Amazingly the universe has given us opportunities time and time again to fail, and just when we think we can't go on any longer, the sun rises and the awakening happens.

The following is a collection of 365 days of affirmations and reflections that have been prayerfully and thoughtfully chosen. I have included balanced and thought-provoking messages that have worked for me on a particular day, regarding a specific challenge. I believe that if you are reading this now, we're sharing a common journey and the pages to follow will speak to you, as they did to me. How you handle your life is relative to your vision, your situation, and your perspective. *Always Balanced and Connected: Daily Affirmations for Body, Mind, and Spirit* is a collection of contemplative thoughts that can guide you away from what your unbalanced self might be seeking. *Always Balanced and Connected: Daily Affirmations for Body, Mind, and Spirit* is designed to give you a new, thought-provoking perspective for the day or perhaps a thought you've had before that could stand repeating. My hope is that the following words of reflection and contemplation will be a source of discovery for you.

Blessings and grace to you on your journey.
Always remember that you are valued and loved.
-Maggie

Author's note: If you are involved in destructive patterns, such as drinking to excess or depending on substances, or you find yourself in an abusive relationship, seek help. If your life or the life of someone you love is out of balance and is suffering, *there is help available.* If you or someone in your life is hurting, *there is help available.* We all need strength and courage to endure in difficult times. For help and assistance, go to "Help" at the back of the book for information. Please note that anything written in this publication is not to replace qualified directive medical or behavioral health diagnosis, evaluation, and treatment.

January

National Mentoring Month

January 1

Affirmation: Today I will think joyous, balanced, and connected thoughts.

Today is the first day of *Always Balanced and Connected*. Am I always balanced and connected? Honestly, no. I do, however, strive to balance my emotions, thoughts, and feelings and stay connected to the positive, loving people, places, and things in my life that work for my good.

I maintain balance as much as possible each day, because I have to. We all have to. When our lives are out of balance, we suffer.

You may not be aware that your life is out of balance. You may not even realize why you're suffering. The truth is, when something in your life isn't where it needs it to be, your thoughts, feelings, and actions are no longer authentic. You're not being true to yourself.

I practice balance in my life, because I have no alternative. I experience imbalance in my life from time to time, and it doesn't work for me.

I have no easy answers for staying in the moment and doing my best. I do, however, have knowledge of and appreciation for those who find themselves feeling not quite right; unable to be the person they know they really are.

Knowing yourself and being truly honest aren't easy tasks. They take deep self-exploration, the desire to let go of what's not working, and faith in yourself, others, and the world around you. They take trust, knowledge, openness, and even a willingness to fail.

January 2

Affirmation: Today I will prepare for what I want to do next.

Living your life in the present is the key to happiness. Strive to be happy with what you have now and thankful that you've been blessed. Try not to look back, and try not to project into the future. Stay in the moment. Take everything one day at a time. "Bloom where you're planted" (Mary Engelbreit).

But what about your dreams, goals, and aspirations? What about the triumphs and mistakes you've made in the past? Don't they count? Learn from your past, but don't get stuck in it. Plan for the future, but don't live for it.

Be prepared, and be ambitious. Know what's required, and be certain to have at your disposal what it takes to get to where you want to be. Goals and objectives are the keys to success. What is it that you want to do, and what do you have to do to get there?

When you live your life your way, you live an authentic life, a life designed specifically for you. Give yourself time, and be patient while working, changing, and growing. Don't expect progress to just show up, and don't think that your situation will always be the same.

Have faith that the future holds many hopes, dreams, and possibilities for you. Regret means feeling sad, angry, or disappointed. Don't let that be an option. Go forward in your life. Take calculated risks. This is your year to shine.

January 3

Affirmation: Today I will recognize the conformity in my life.

It takes courage to go against popular belief. It takes courage to stand up for equality or speak up against violence. It takes courage to speak your truth when it's not socially acceptable to do so.

You conform in more ways than you realize. Cowardice in conformity is when you do what's expected of you even though it goes against what you hold sacred. Conformity is at its peak when you follow along, doing what's expected of you simply because that's the way it's always been.

Be aware of what's important to you personally. Always be true to your own values and passions. Know your limitations, and know when you're willing to expand your boundaries. Be authentic, and live out loud. Future generations are counting on you.

January 4

Affirmation: Today I will acknowledge that I often say and do things I think others want me to.

Conflicts, confusion, and misunderstandings are unnecessary when you're true to yourself. When you do or say what other people want or expect you to, you don't represent what's true and real about yourself.

When you act the way you think people want you to act, you become a people pleaser. To be a true people pleaser, you have to try to please everyone all the time. If you have a modicum of intelligence, you know this isn't possible. But to a true people pleaser, it's vital.

The need to be liked and loved is a coping mechanism. Pleasing people and making them happy speaks to the need to have everyone like you. It means you care about what others think of you. It's a way of life for many. Needing everyone to like you is a means of suppressing fear, pain, and anxiety. *If anyone really knew me, they wouldn't like me.* It's a quest to never disappoint, upset, or anger anyone at all costs.

Does this ring true for you or someone you love? The goal of a people pleaser is to never, under any circumstances, give anyone cause to not like you. Not only is it impossible for everyone to like you, it's inauthentic and emotionally draining.

The need to please everyone causes anger, resentment, and inner turmoil. You're not bringing to life anything that's uniquely you. Your own thoughts and likes are suppressed and never see the light of day. What you were put on this planet to accomplish or contribute may never manifest. You end up living a less-than-authentic life. You end up living someone else's life. Or worse, you end up living everybody else's life, whether it's good or bad.

January 5

Affirmation: Today I will take the helpful ideas of others to heart for my own good.

Do you reject or have you given up on anything that has to do with religion, spirituality, or energy outside yourself? Have you been jaded by a personal or family history with your faith? Is there a part of you that you're unable or unwilling to get in touch with—your spirit or your soul perhaps?

Some people may mistakenly think that faith or spirituality is about religion, but faith allows you to believe that things will work out without your having to control everything. Let go and surrender to a will greater than yourself. Practicing your faith encourages and teaches you how to be the best person you can be.

Live simply and with your best intention for yourself and others. That's living spiritually. That's living a faith-based life—living a life where love outweighs hatred. There's no need to worry. Life is filled with possibilities. Be open-minded and openhearted.

January 6

Affirmation: Today I will replace all negative thoughts with a different, more enlightened viewpoint.

How easy is it for you to think badly about someone? How easy is it to be negative when you've been hurt over and over again? Do you choose to be unhappy because being happy is just too much work? When I ask a child, "Is it easier to act badly or to act well?" he or she inevitably responds, "It's easier to act well!"

You know that with wisdom and experience, those sentiments can change, and it becomes much easier to act badly at times. In fact, it's hard to act well.

We all act poorly to differing degrees. Saying that someone is stupid is acting badly. Eating an entire bag of cookies is a poor choice. Acting badly is choosing to do wrong and failing to do right.

Notice I say "acting" badly. You're not bad; the choices you make are bad.

It's easy to put people down, judge them, or even bully them, because, in the short run, you feel better about yourself. It's easy to take something that doesn't belong to you at work, because no one will know and because they won't miss it anyway. It's easy to be unfaithful, because you're not loved at home.

Maintaining balance is doing what you know to be in your own best interest and in the interest of those you care about. Balance—not perfection or failure—is the goal.

Making strong, healthy choices that work for you is the best possible course of action. Giving up lying, cheating, and being negative at whatever level, as often as possible, is the driving force to becoming the best person you can be.

We all do things that either work or don't work for us in the moment. You know what you must start doing and stop doing to realize your own good choices and decisions in life. Give up the bad in your life, and you'll feel such a strong release and a burden will be lifted. Well done!

January 7

Affirmation: Today I will think in a loving, kind, and charitable way.

Do you want to think of yourself as helpful or smart? Do you want to think of yourself as an amazing caretaker or a person who's trustworthy? The simplicity of "you are what you think" is the best. It's a no-brainer!

The problem with wisdom is that the more basic the concept, the more difficult it can be to comprehend. Think about what's complicated in your life. Give up 50 percent of the nonessentials in your life, and therein lies your bliss.

The problem is that you're taught to try to accomplish more, obtain more, gather more, and be more. Try letting go. Pare down your stuff; get rid of the physical and emotional clutter in your life. Strive to be good enough instead of the best, and live simply. The less you have, the less you have to worry about and take care of. Perhaps less can be better.

January 8

Affirmation: I have immeasurable potential.

As we begin a new year, many of us set out to change unwanted behaviors. Give up a sugar addiction, get to the gym, and quit smoking are the most popular New Year's resolutions. At any time throughout the year, what we really need to do is focus on what we want to start doing. Set goals, prioritize those goals, and figure out the necessary steps to obtain our goals. Overeating and smoking are distractions some use to make themselves feel better in the moment. Some overeat because of feelings of inadequacy or loneliness. Some continue to use nicotine for fear of not being able to break the addiction. When we change our circumstances to meet our new goals and accomplishments and to be where we want to be, we no longer need to rely on vices to give ourselves a temporary fix.

Every beginning is a new opportunity to start fresh. I resolve daily to be smarter, to be kinder, to be more loving, and to live my life authentically.

January 9

Affirmation: Today I will go through the day with a beginner's mind-set.

Throughout our lives we strive to be proficient in everything we do. We want to excel. We want to be on top. However, in order to get there, we must start at the very beginning. There are no shortcuts to success. There is no jumping ahead in line. There is no buying our way to the top.

Some people would like to think that's a reality, but in the true greatness of sports, business, and the arts, it is those who started at the beginning, with a beginner's mind-set, who truly master their craft. Oftentimes you see people who have raw talent and can belt out an aria with little to no effort. This is rare. People rarely pick up a thought or idea and master it instantaneously. When faced with a new idea or challenge, some of us pass it by or do not go for it because of insecurities or fear of embarrassment. You don't want to admit to it, or you don't want others to see you as a beginner. It is much better to see a beginner at the gym than a person who has mastered the art of sitting on the couch. Leave your ego at the door, and go for that tap-dancing class or Surfing 101. At some point, you will go from a beginner's mind-set to mastery.

January 10

Affirmation: Today I will make new mistakes.

Be in the moment. Yesterday's gone, and tomorrow is not here. All you have is today. Being in the moment is living authentically. When you look back on the choices you've made in the past, it's common to obsess about all the things you've done wrong. Do you have unfinished business with a friend, colleague, or family member? Do you want a second chance to say or do things differently? What you did in the past has made you the person you are—a stronger person than you may think.

Looking back, were there also good times? Were there times of reward and achievement, celebration and happiness? The good times are there to guide you through troubled waters.

When looking back over your life, ask yourself, "What was my intention at the time?" In moments of solitude, do you regurgitate, reinvent, and tend to remember memories as good or bad?

Trying to do better next time is the best way to learn from your past. Memories hold a strong, tight grip at times and can have a power over you if you let them. However, your past can make you stronger in your words, deeds, and thoughts. When you look back, give yourself the freedom to do so with a loving mind and open heart. When you plan your future, do it with happiness and joy. Just recognize that you will make new mistakes.

January 11

Affirmation: Today I will let a lot go.

Looking through fashion magazines can lead to feelings of envy and jealousy. Beautiful houses, beautiful models, big boats, hundreds of articles on ways to improve your swing in every issue of *Golf Digest*—everything in the media is geared toward how you can be better, how you can improve, and how you can be perfect. Perfection is a disease, however. Why is it so important to be perfect? Wanting to be the best could be a result of childhood. The need to be perfect may be self-propelled; however a person comes to being a perfectionist, rest assured that, contrary to popular belief, it's not a healthy obsession.

True and honest perfection is being whole and complete, while being able to make mistakes and learn from them. It's being comfortable with who, what, where, and why you are who you are now. However, *comfortable* does not have to be *complacent*. The key to balance is acknowledging your flaws and shortcomings and being open to change. There is improvement to be made for everyone, but the end goal is not to be the biggest, brightest, richest, and most successful at all costs. Being humble yet proud of yourself and your achievements can be more satisfying in the long run.

Striving for perfection in a destructive way, can promote a critical heart. Having someone in your life that always wants you to be something different from who you are has the potential to develop into sheer misery. It can break down self-esteem and erode any sense of mastery.

What is healthy and promotes joy, kindness, and understanding is taking a complete inventory of you. Look at what is possible. Look at what can be different, what you know you would like to work on and do for you, not for anyone else. Put away the magazines for a while, and live your life—warts and all! Look past the imperfections, and focus on what is possible.

January 12

Affirmation: Today I will be fully present.

Do you feel like yourself most days? Do you speak your truth, or do you give only partially of who you really are? Every day is a new opportunity to be who you are truly meant to be. Are you funny yet afraid to show your humorous side? Are you romantic but keep that side to yourself, thinking it's uncomfortable for you to show affection or act romantically? Do you have unanswered questions that you are afraid to ask, for fear of embarrassment or rejection?

Society has a strong hold on us. It wants us to act a certain way, to fit a certain type, to fit in. If you watch others while you could be a participant, you are not truly living the life you were meant to live. True joy and happiness can be passing you by, and this is not what the creator has in mind for you. God wants you to seize the moment. When you feel like singing, turn up the volume and belt it out. This does not mean you can do whatever you want to do anytime or anywhere.

Here's when the gift of balance comes into play. Understanding what's in your best interest and in the interest of those who care about you is acting out of love. If you're going to hurt or embarrass someone with your thoughts, deeds, or actions, stop, and take a moment to reconsider. If you come from a loving place, where you can bring out your talents, knowledge, and passion, take every opportunity to soar.

January 13

Affirmation: Today when I share beauty or joy with someone, I will know that I have a partner in love, a partner in God.

When you look at a gorgeous sunset or sit beside a calm, peaceful river, you feel happiness. When witnessing the beauty of a night sky, you may want to shout out to others,

"Come see!" And then you find yourself stopping and wanting the moment only for yourself. When alone, the beauty is a deep, internal joy; when shared with others, it is infectious. Millions of beachgoers camp out on their blankets, waiting all day for the sun to set. The beauty is undeniable, but what is this attraction to the ever-changing dance of light and color? What is it about the sun going down that fills us with awe? Scientifically, sunsets, as well as sunrises, signify the continuing movement of the earth and the planets. Spiritually they cry out that there is a force of nature much greater than us to be reckoned with. It is the handwork of a graceful brushstroke that's always brilliant and always unique. The beauty signals yet another day and ends in the security of knowing that we have another chance tomorrow to do it all again. Optimism and the promise of the possibilities of a new day will be shared. When you find that beauty today, share the feeling with another who just might need to be lifted spiritually and emotionally. Always keep in mind how you can bring joy to those around you.

January 14

Affirmation: I do know. I always know.

You *do* know. Prayer and meditation will bring the answers to your questions to the surface if you take the time to listen. There is no greater authority over your life than you. When you were a child, you looked to your parents, your teachers, and your friends for answers to your questions. However, in your adult life, there comes a time when you take ownership of your thoughts, actions, and feelings. It's no longer up to your mom or dad what you have for lunch.

Whether or not you went to college, or work, or enlisted in the military was probably the first major life decision you made as a young adult. If that decision didn't turn out right for you or a decision you made early on in your life failed, you might give up on thinking that you are in control of your own future and do what you think others want or expect you to do. In actuality, it's possibly the failed choices that make your life decisions easier moving forward. Missed opportunities can teach you what it is you want and what it is you don't want out of life.

Today I will take a moment to ponder the questions and gently, silently, and patiently wait for the answers.

January 15

Affirmation: Today I will speak the truth and live my life in honesty and love.

The truth will set you free when you are in accord with the body of real things, real events, and actualities. It's alignment. It means that when you speak the truth, you are balanced and don't have to overcompensate or change your direction or intention to modify what is.

When you say yes when you mean yes and no when you mean no, you're being authentic. When you tell it like it is, you're being real. There are, of course, those nasty little gray areas known as "little white lies" or half-truths. Is it okay to lie? Everyone lies. Omitting the truth or keeping information from someone is akin to lying. All children and adults grapple with the truth. *If I tell the truth, I will get in trouble. If I tell a lie, no one will know.* This type of thinking can graduate into a dishonest lifestyle and being the type of person who cannot be trusted.

When in doubt, tread lightly with the truth, as you would a fragile feather. Speak it softly and slowly until it gains momentum. Then let go and watch your words take flight. Being dishonest is a bad habit, and it can easily be given up for the truth. When the truth hurts, hold back. When someone is called upon to be the champion of what's right, stand up. It will become a way of life through knowledge, peace, and inner strength. Today I will choose honesty no matter how difficult.

January 16

Affirmation: Today I will compliment my loved ones and a total stranger!

I feel great when I am complimented. Doesn't everyone? Not always. Not everyone. It can be hard for some people. It's hard for many people.

When you see someone doing something wonderful, come out of your shell and let them know how inspiring they are—yes, even if it's a total stranger. Don't miss these opportunities to let God's grace flow through you.

Perhaps you were raised in a family where there wasn't a lot of praise to go around. All it would have taken for your inner child to be comforted was to hear, "Good job," or "You're the best!" Hopefully, the idea of letting people know they're appreciated and valued will gain momentum. It builds strong character and positive self-esteem. Being truly loved and appreciated means you are the recipient of a sufficient amount of outward signs of love and affirmation. You need to be shown that you are loved. If you are not the recipient of praise and compliments from others, by all means compliment yourself every day, and know that you matter.

January 17

Affirmation: Today I will be open to a miracle in my life.

Miracles happen. They don't have to be earth-shattering. Miracles come in all sizes. The hand of Spirit may intervene in a person's life or in a situation that otherwise seems futile or impossible. When you experience the truest, most wonderful feeling in the world, that is a miracle, a wonder, a marvel.

Today, take the time to think about and reflect on the miracles in your life up until now—marrying a loving spouse, graduating from school when perhaps you were heading in the wrong direction, getting through a difficult time in your life, being surrounded by a loving and supportive family, making a decent living, or giving birth to a child. Life that is born of love is a true miracle.

When disappointment sets in and life is not going the way you want it to or life continues to be a struggle, wake up each morning and expect a miracle. Be open and receptive. Your miracle will come. If you keep an open heart, you will receive your blessing for the day. The more you anticipate miracles to happen, the more they will appear when most needed. Some people say that things will turn out fine in the end. If your life is not where you want it to be now, then perhaps you're not at the end.

January 18

Affirmation: Today I will pay attention.

Only you can determine the quality of your life. The quantity of years we live is yet to be determined. No one knows for certain how long we are here for. However, how you live your life and how you choose to design your own destiny is within your reach. Your personal hopes, dreams, aspirations, goals, and skills construct the path that is yours exclusively.

To what degree do you give your attention to the people in your life, to the subtleties of what is in front of you at any given moment? The nuances of being alive are often overlooked. The dew on the rose and the vibrant colors of a tiger's coat are what matter in nature and in life. Today, pay attention to that which you would most likely pass by.

January 19

Affirmation: I belong.

We all belong, at one time or another, to a family, an organization, or a group. We all belong to the human race. It's common to feel disconnected to self, to others, or to God. Feeling inadequate or like you don't fit in is scary and anxiety producing for a large percent of the population. You may be different from the other people in your circles. You may be one of the people who feel disconnected. You feel as though you don't fit in with the people around you, as though they have something you don't have or they are in some way better than you. This skewed thinking comes from a judgmental and self-deprecating place. Whether you believe it or not, that thinking is self-imposed. The truth is you do belong. Everyone brings their own talents and unique selves to any situation. The unique qualities and talents that you have are yours alone; no one else is exactly like you. No friends are identical. Families are as diversified as can be.

You think that in order to belong, you must assimilate. You must compromise. You must give in to fit in. Standing out in a crowd is a beautiful alternative to feeling small and not good enough. How then is it possible to be connected to something or someone and remain true to your authentic self?

Chances are that if you are feeling judged on the way you look or the clothes you wear, you just might be a person who is judgmental too! Stop judging, period. Live and let live. Gay, straight, all colors, all creeds—all men and women are meant to be here. Let us live together and help each other belong by celebrating life and love with all their beauty. Today, celebrate what makes you unique.

January 20

Affirmation: Today I will think positively.

You truly can determine your feelings and actions with your thoughts. Changing the way you think changes the way you feel and act. Changes in the way you act will change the way you think and feel. Changes in the way you feel ... well, you get it. It's all integrated. It's the body–mind–spirit connection at work. If you think you are amazing, and if you think you are talented, you are! It is amazing to know that whatever you choose to do is possible just by beginning to think about it.

Many people with "bad attitudes" proclaim to be just fine that way. Young girls and guys think it's cool to call each other derogatory names. Behaving badly and demeaning others have the potential to perpetuate animosity.

However, when you start putting forth positive thoughts, you are not shielded from experiencing pain and defeat. Some people fail to continue on and give up trying. It's easier to quit and not believe in yourself. Giving in to negativity is easier than continuing on until you reach your goal. Reaching your goal takes work. Believe that your dreams will come true, and have patience.

Thinking positively is extremely hard for anyone who grew up in a home where self-awareness and self-esteem were not nurtured. Many families are dysfunctional because of drugs, alcohol, or abuse. Growing up in a family where dreams are not encouraged or realized can make it difficult, or nearly impossible, to believe that your happiness is up to you. Break the cycle of negativity, and walk the path to knowing that if you think it can happen, it just might.

January 21

Affirmation: Today I will work on togetherness in my private and professional life.

Achievement and accomplishment—in terms of total concentration, a spirit of togetherness, and strength—are vital for success. There always will be relationships that can be better. Togetherness is vital to being truly happy. Having people in your life whom you hate, are estranged from, don't talk to, or simply can't stand affects *you*. One way to improve your health and wellness is to be the best person you can be, and that means being the best person you can be toward others. The fact is that there's always a price to pay if you harbor resentment toward another person in your heart. You become preoccupied with negativity and hate. Be all right with others, and you'll have a clear path to be able to focus and give your all.

Strength is also a prerequisite for achievement. Strength is being able to be cooperative and get along with someone who is unapologetic. Strength is working side by side with people with whom you are angry or even with those you despise. Should you not hate or be angry with everyone? That is the ultimate goal, but for now the first step is to be tolerant and non-antagonistic. Take "hate" out of your vocabulary, and work on a spirit of togetherness. It is all about the end of the journey.

January 22

Affirmation: Today I will not hide behind my secrets.

Not telling the whole truth about yourself to yourself or to loved ones is basically hiding behind your secrets. Everybody has secrets. It's true. We all keep things from others and live with what we don't want others to know. We are human, and we are flawed. As we age we realize the consequences of keeping our thoughts, feelings, and actions of the past bottled up inside. If you are on a path to improving yourself emotionally and spiritually, you must stop yourself from withholding what you feel you must never let go of, if at all possible.

Keeping what others have told you in strict confidence to yourself is a virtue, and it is very hard to do. Trust me. Being cautious with whom you share your secrets is also extremely difficult. It requires complete trust in your confidant. Clergy, doctors, attorneys, counselors, and psychotherapists are professional "secret keepers."

January 23

Affirmation: Today I will free myself of the chaos in my life.

Freedom means being free of something or someone, being released. True freedom is when you are in a place of calmness, are aware of yourself and your surroundings, and have an open heart to new possibilities. Does this mean you have to be in a Zen state to achieve freedom? Perhaps it means you must strive to learn the skills and techniques required to be in a place where you're able to be calm and aware of your thoughts, feelings, and actions. Take a minute to think of how you run around, day in and day out, putting out fires. Or perhaps you run on empty, going from one activity to another. Maybe your desk at work is overloaded with unfinished tasks, and your inbox is full.

True freedom is being in a place where the chaos of the world or even the chaos in your life does not impede your happiness. Try letting the chaos go. It's a way of life that is not good for anyone. Chaos prevents you from having the goodness in your life override the stress and strife. Worry and fear create a constant confused and spiraling-out-of-control way of life. Strive daily to cultivate your faith in God, your faith in people, your faith in the universe, and your faith in yourself. Chaos is managed with prayer or meditation.

Today, I will take a moment to calm the chaos in my life. All is well. I will pause to be present and trust that all is as it should be.

January 24

Affirmation: I am the best I can be in this moment.

Every day is a new day. Every moment is an opportunity for change. The only moment you have control over is the present moment. In this moment you are the best you can be. Circumstances change, attitudes change, and the future is yet to be determined. Perhaps you suffer guilt due to bad judgment calls and mistakes in the past. Projecting negativity only makes you feel that you are inept or less than. The truth is in this very moment you *are* doing your best, even if you are doing nothing. The next moment will come, and you will either go forward in your actions or thoughts, or you will regress, but it will still be the best you can do at that moment. Sometimes life gets in the way, moods change, circumstances change, and people change. In this moment you need to set a standard for yourself, and if you feel you are not moving in the direction of your goals, you must reevaluate change. But for now, you are good enough.

January 25

Affirmation: Today I will let go of what doesn't matter.

Anxiety and depression can absolutely be chemically based. Having said that, depression and anxiety can be managed if you get to the root of the issue, make a plan to let go of the negativity surrounding it, and make changes in your thoughts and actions. Anxiety is fear based, and depression can be anger turned inward. Both of these emotional ailments can be addressed by talking out your thoughts and feelings. Holding onto your pride or fear of embarrassment or failure can be dealt with with right thinking. There is no judgment associated with right thinking. Right thinking pertains to what is right for you and only you. You know what is right for you, and when you are not following the messages that are helpful and productive, anxiety exists. When you are not right thinking and project feelings of hatred, remorse, and jealousy, you can feel depressed.

Letting go of anything that does not work for you will promote health and wellness. You know who you are at your best. You know what is right for you and how you are on your best day. You are a loving, kind, and caring child of God.

January 26

Affirmation: Life is good.

You have only scratched the surface of your potential. Whatever age you are, now is the right time. Whatever situation you are in, look for the potential for growth and greatness. Gather what you need. Find the right people who will support your efforts. Plan your journey, and take the first step. If that step feels right, take another and then another. Practice positive affirmations to help you strive to reach your full potential in life.

We all get to a point when we are tired and worn-out. When you are feeling down on yourself, take time to regroup. Being overwrought is an indication that you've been working too hard and are overstressed. Give yourself a break. Be kind to yourself and others. Think about what it is you are doing that you could do differently, and then get back in the game. Life is full of potential. Life is good.

January 27

Affirmation: Today I will cultivate faith in someone.

Having faith in someone just might be a life-changing experience. It has the potential to change the course of whom you trust, as well. What's holding your faith hostage? We all need to know we are honored and loved. We need to know there are people in our lives who know us, trust us, and believe in us. We all need someone in our corner.

Faith in something or someone encourages growth, change, and success. Think back on the people and places that encouraged you along the way. Where would you be if not for that certain someone believing in you and guiding you? If you didn't have someone in your corner, perhaps you recognize how difficult it is for you to go it alone. Believing in and encouraging someone does a body good. Have faith in someone before he or she is successful.

Faith is guidance given to you on alternative routes on your journey with the divine. What you do with your life depends on your own, very specific, set of circumstances. Decide who you are now, physically, mentally, and emotionally. Take a look at who is in your life right now. Do you have faith in them? Do they need you to pray for them? Do you need to pray with them? Faith in others and yourself produces loving thoughts of kindness, encouragement, praise, and peace. I have faith in the power of goodness and love.

January 28

Affirmation: It is good to be generous.

The best thing to do if you're feeling poor is to give something away. Give a few dollars to a homeless person or donate some clothes to a thrift shop. Instead of focusing on what you don't have, focus on what you do have and how you can bless others with it. Being able to give is a divine gift.

It's not up to us to determine others' needs. If you choose to give to only those who appear to be in need on the outside, you are discounting all the others who may seemingly have everything but have not felt human kindness or have not been given anything in a very long time. Try giving gifts to people for no special reason. Intend to be kind, and show compassion to others. Take time out of your busy life to create something of joy and uniqueness for someone else. Make that person's day better.

January 29

Affirmation: I will begin today with prayer.

Prayer is simply talking to Spirit. Spirit is what gives you strength, courage, and the will to be the best person you can be. It is the source that allows you to eliminate negativity and pain from your life. This sacred energy creeps into your life to free you from control of all things at all times. When you pray, you get in touch with the part of your life that transcends thoughts and actions. You connect with an energy that brings light and goodness into your life. It's easy to start the day in a negative frame of mind. The alarm clock is obnoxious, and you have to leave the house at a ridiculous time to beat the traffic. Or you might have to get the kids up and out. Or what if you wake up and you're feeling lonely?

Before the excitement of the day, before you get out of bed, pray, talk to God and ask for guidance, be thankful, and know that nothing is going to happen today that you and God can't handle together. When you begin your day by communing with the divine, you are spiritually fortified. Your days will overflow with grace.

January 30

Affirmation: I use my time and talents to help others.

Whether you know it or not, you have many passions, talents, and gifts. Pursuit of happiness—in the form of developing your personal talent (that thing that you can do that is unique to you)—is good for the soul. Following your heart and doing the things that make you happy provide much needed therapy, as well.

Fear of success or failure can prohibit you from trying new things. Low self-esteem also makes it hard to try something new. When you are stressed or overwhelmed, you tell yourself it's not a good time right now. However, now is always the best time.

Your accomplishments don't have to be satisfying to only you. You are blessed so that others can enjoy your efforts too. It's extremely gratifying when you give of yourself to help someone else. Can you give a gift certificate for cooking classes to a charity benefit, or can you sing or play the piano at an event? Making someone else's life easier, by saying, "Yes, I'm willing to give back," provides an amazing feeling. Bringing joy to others has the power to bring you the happiness you need to continue on your way.

I am highly enthusiastic, overjoyed, and amazed by what I have been able to do so far with the talents with which I have been blessed. If this sentiment doesn't ring true for you, it's possible you have untapped talents you don't even know exist. What is it that you think you might want to try? You probably have hidden talents you never knew you had, and all you have to do is go for it. You'll be shocked and amazed at how easy your skill will come to you. Others will notice too.

It's time to unleash your inner dancer, artist, singer, woodworker, or comedian. Become a gourmet cook, crafter, potter, beekeeper, hiker, organic farmer, or candlestick maker. Be inspired, be committed, be willing to try, and, most importantly, be amazed!

January 31

Affirmation: Today I will take a giant step toward my future.

I am thinking about taking my career to the next level. I want to try something new; something I have never done before. I want to meet new people. I am ready to travel. Today, give yourself permission to plan a new goal, a new dream or a new direction for your life. (If you are happy exactly where you are, in this moment, there is no need to make dramatic plans for the future.) But for most of us, the status quo, our existing state of affairs, particularly with regards to our social life or life outside the home could use some changing or rearranging every now and then.

What is keeping you from trying new things? Low self-esteem or lack of support from friends and family can make it hard to try something new. When you are stressed or overwhelmed, you may tell yourself it's not a good time right now. However, now is always the best time. Your desire to find your calling is on your mind and in your heart at this very moment.

When we make changes to better our circumstances, others will enjoy our efforts, as well. When you take off in the direction of fulfilling your purpose in life, you might just wake up one morning and witness how much you are better for it and how much your improvements are helping others. It will produce an amazing feeling. Bringing joy to others has the power to bring you the happiness you need to continue on your way. It's extremely gratifying to know that you're on *your* path to joy and happiness.

February

Black History Month

February 1

Affirmation: I am a trailblazer.

Are you a leader or a follower? It's certainly more challenging to be a leader. Following the pack is the path of least resistance. Doing your own thing and going your own way are not only more satisfying and rewarding, but they make you unique.

When we're young, the "rebel spirit" is infectious. Young people like to either stand out or comply with an agreed upon set of rules. Being authentic is a constant balancing act between when to fit in and when to stand out at any age.

To be unique—one of a kind, colorful, outrageous, uncensored, and brilliant—is to know who you are and what you want. It is knowing that you have something special to offer. Not only is it inspiring when you realize that you're amazing, but it is also a blessing when knowing what you do with your talents and how you continue to contribute throughout your life is amazing.

When you resist the urge to be daring, you sign on for conformity. It's an existence that might suit your needs, but it will never exceed your expectations. That sounds like something we all have to face in our lives.

February 2

Affirmation: Today I will accept my life the way it is.

Accepting yourself as you are is huge. Accepting the people you love in life is crucial. The more you try to change people, the more difficult the relationship becomes.

In the beginning you ignore what is bothering you about your loved ones. You may be in denial. Then slowly you graduate to pointing out their faults to them. You think that telling them what is wrong with them is going to help. You buy CD's and audio books trying to get information on how to change the other person, to no avail. You become abrasive. You consider leaving the relationship. You try to decide whether or not the people you love mean more to you than their shortcomings.

What you once loved in your partner perhaps you now detest. What is your next strategy? You've run out of ideas. Accept your loved one for who he or she is right now. You cannot change anything until you accept it. As long as he or she is not hurting you or anyone else, work with how he or she is acting. Condemning others can perhaps prohibit them from ever changing. Sarcasm and name-calling are for bullies. Bullying is crippling. Putting people down doesn't help; it oppresses. Keep in mind that you can only change how you feel and how you act. How liberating is that for everyone involved?

February 3

Affirmation: I will relinquish my need to have power over those I love.

Power is a word that some people think of fondly and others don't. It depends on how power is used. In relationships with those we love, power has no place. Trying to one-up each other or having to prove you are right is futile. Both people end up hurting. Having power over our children is also a losing battle. Power is turned off and on with the flip of a switch. Instead of wanting to be powerful, strive for wanting to be successful, caring, and loving.

There are times, however, when power is a good thing. Power can be a strong characteristic when it comes to having power over your own destiny. *I feel strong and powerful in body, mind, and spirit today.* The acquisition and acceptance of power for individual growth and improvement must not be confused with overpowering others in the process. It may be a fine line to distinguish. Temper the need for power with balance in your life.

February 4

Affirmation: The earth knows what it needs to do and so do I.

Winter is a season that perhaps few people look forward to, February especially! Winter is tough. Some people go to great lengths to relocate to warm climates for health purposes or for personal enjoyment. What most folks who live in the northern regions are privy to is that it is known to be a time to "make the best of a difficult situation." Sure there is a huge population of skiers, snow boarders, hikers and kids of all ages who long for snow and cold weather. When I say tough I am referring to snowy roads, icy sidewalks, sleet, chilly winds, temperatures in the single digits, losing heat and hot water during a snowstorm or being stranded when your car won't start. All this is universal to anyone who has a history with colder climates. The earth's movement around the sun causes the seasons. This basic fact helps me tremendously on a cold winter day. It tells me that all is as it should be. The earth is working! Thinking about the earth's movement around the sun as part of a growing season gets me through the long winter months happily and joyfully. Winter brings spring. The earth tilts away from the sun in winter. For six months in the summer it is tilted toward the sun. This is a metaphor for humans to tilt away from the sun for a period of time in order to restore, to renew and to grow!

February 5

Affirmation: I can do better.

Every day is a new day. Every moment is an opportunity to change. The only moment over which you have control is the present moment you are experiencing. In this moment you can strive to do better. Circumstances change, attitudes change, and the future is yet to be determined.

Perhaps you are guilt ridden by bad judgments and mistakes in the past, and they cloud the *now*. Projecting only makes you feel that you are inept or less than. The next moment will come, and either you will go forth in your actions and thoughts or you will regress. The key is to try to be better than you are now.

Change won't happen if you don't do things differently. Circumstances and changes in awareness will propel you to either change or go down even further, but in the moment you will rise to the level that you can. When you are doing well and moving in a positive direction, good for you! Keep the momentum going.

You will not always be happy. Life gets in the way, moods change, circumstances change, and people change. In this moment set a standard, and if you feel that you are not moving in the direction of your goals, re-evaluate and set clear and consistent objectives. Enjoy the moment. Enjoy the day.

February 6

Affirmation: Today I will encourage someone.

How much do you know that others aren't aware of? There is a wealth of information that you can get from computers, iPads, iPhones, and so on, yet the true essence of knowledge and wisdom is within you. Yes, even if you are eight or ninety-eight, you have something to give others in the way of encouragement, support, unconditional love, and acceptance. If you are feeling down or particularly hard on yourself, that is when it is most difficult to encourage someone, yet this is the time you must. It's when you put yourself, your troubles, and your woes aside and focus on the plight of another that you truly wake up from your sleep to the possibility of hope, kindness, and understanding. A fundamental desire in relationships is to be heard and understood. Today, be the best person for someone else, and know that it matters. You benefit by lifting others.

February 7

Affirmation: I will acknowledge love.

I am so small compared to the sea, the sky, and the earth. I am small compared to the vastness of the universe. The earth is mine to preserve and protect. My job is to love the earth and the environment.

What sets us apart as a human race is the ability to love and empathize. You are nothing without love. Love determines strength of character. You are called on to be part of the human family. One thing is clear: love is the driving force. Love bears all, and only love can conquer hate. Love is a feeling, an emotion, and a powerful force beyond words. Love is also a choice in the absence of feelings. Love your neighbor, love your family, and, most of all, love yourself. The trials and tribulations of life are bearable only through love.

February 8

Affirmation: How I think determines my mood.

If you think and act happy, your mood will improve. Certainly no one can dispute that. Sometimes it's hard to realize that you have control over your feelings. Your feelings, thoughts, and actions are either in sync or they are working against you. It's up to you. No one (and nothing) else can determine how your day is going to go.

When you're upset or angry, perhaps you think it's because of something someone else said or did. You are mad and frustrated because of the aggressive drivers on the road. You blame your boss for stressing you out. You have the power to change your mood. Don't blame anything or anyone else. You're in control by how you interpret events and the meaning you place on them.

You might be the type of person who turns to substances to make you feel better, when, in fact, they don't make you feel better; they make you feel worse. Self-indulgence is often a means of coping with your feelings.

Remember—you create your own joy or sadness by changing your thoughts. The way you think affects how you feel and how you act. You are also in control of your stress level and your overall health and wellness. When you are at peace, you are happy. Happiness is when you are in harmony with what is going on around you, when you are peaceful.

February 9

Affirmation: I will let go of the need to hear the words "I'm sorry."

Some people say they will forgive, but they will never forget. Others say that you can't forgive unless you forget. Forgiveness is ongoing, and once you forgive someone, you must work toward rebuilding the relationship to include trust and mutual respect. If you can't get to that place, agree to disagree and move on. Do not harbor resentment. You can forgive someone even though you don't ever tell him or her. You can forgive that person in your heart. It is never too late.

When you choose not to forgive someone, you give that person control over your thoughts and emotions. You remain an emotional hostage. Perhaps the other person is unaware of what he or she did and just how much he or she hurt you. Perhaps his or her intention was not to hurt you at all. Perhaps there was a misunderstanding. Consider the other person might be having a difficult time in his or her life or is in need of love or attention. So much goes on behind what you feel is an assault or an injustice against you. It is not so much what people say or do that hurts; it is how they made you feel. I know. Try, just for today, to accept an apology you never got.

February 10

Affirmation: Today I will let go of my anger and give forgiveness a try.

To be at peace, you must first let go of negativity and forgive. Forgiveness may seem simple. We learned it as a child. However, forgiveness is extremely difficult when you feel personally offended or violated.

It's so hard to forgive when the person you need to forgive has not recognized what he or she did to you. The person you need to forgive has never said he or she is sorry. How can you forgive when the person who has hurt you doesn't even acknowledge that what he or she did was wrong?

Change the way you think about that person and the situation that is plaguing you. Challenge your thoughts about the matter. Try thinking differently than you have in the past, or try adjusting your perspective on the hurt and pain you feel right now. When you begin to think differently, it will be much easier to change the way you feel and let go of resentment. Do not give others power over you. Do not be easily offended. Take hardship and misunderstandings with a grain of salt, and move on. Let the anger go. It only harms you. Be forgiving of others, because you deserve peace.

February 11

Affirmation: I will ask for strength today through prayer.

"God, give me strength, courage, and guts." Say this every day. It is not elaborate. It is not flowery. It is not complicated or hard to remember. It is basic and powerful. Throughout your day and throughout your life, you may find yourself scared, anxious, or nervous. It is extremely common. You are not alone. When you take the time to breathe, take a moment for yourself and remember that nothing can or will get done, right or inspired, without calling on your higher power. God will never let you go. How amazing is that! Give prayer a chance. It is powerful, uncomplicated, and wonderful.

February 12

Affirmation: Today I will partner with someone who is like-minded.

We can do so much together. Together we are strong. When we join our hearts, prayers, and intentions with the heart, prayers, and intentions of someone else, almost anything is possible. How many times have you asked someone to get something down from a shelf that you could not reach and he or she was happy to help? Such is life. Why then is it that many find it so difficult to ask for help when faced with life altering situations? Is it perhaps due to fear or shame?

In times of desperation, help is the only prayer we need: "Help me to find my way." "Help me with my struggles." "Help me to provide a life for my family and myself." Are you proud or embarrassed? Are we a society of people who would rather be without than to admit we need help? When we ask for help from loved ones or strangers, we are, in essence, helping them in their journey to be better people. When we seek help, we, in turn, can help others. You begin to realize the importance of giving of your time and talents to others. Helping brings joy and purpose not only to the receiver but also to the provider. "Is there anything I can do to help?" That's all it takes.

February 13

Affirmation: Only generosity will make you rich.

In this world of accumulation and acquisition, it is refreshing to be able to help others when it is not easy or give of yourself, your time, and your talent when it seems like a burden. When you give to others, you get back in other ways.

When you feel like something is missing in your life, think about what is it specifically that you require to realize your authentic self. Essentials such as air, food, shelter and water of course are needed. Beyond that, what do you really need to do the work you are called to do, live the life that makes you most happy or that makes you a better person?

Stop and take a moment to think about what you truly need and require for your happiness. A keyboard to play music or a new apartment because the one you live in no longer meets your needs or maybe it is getting a puppy to love. When we give we receive. Prioritize your needs against others without forgetting yourself in the process. Having a giving spirit is a blessing. When you feel like you may not have everything you want, think about the fact that you just might have what you need.

February 14

Affirmation: True love is when I am loving toward others.

We're all in a constant search for that special kind of love that poets, artists, and writers have been detailing for centuries. It is a feeling that can sustain us throughout our lives. Without love, we are constantly searching for what is missing in our lives. Hope, appreciation, devotion, dedication, and true selflessness are emotions of love that I take with me throughout my life. I can bring these loving feelings with me wherever I go and call on them no matter what I am doing.

Love propels us to move forward in life. Love provides a purpose to be our best selves. It is not who or what you love; it is how deeply and genuinely you give of yourself. In order to be loved, you must give love. When you are feeling lonely and unloved, remember to give to others that which is missing in your life.

February 15

Affirmation: The people in my life know when I am happy. Today I will check in with them from time to time.

Today I will stop focusing on the negative and make a conscious decision to be kind, thankful, and sincere. Being thankful is so important to happiness. On social media there is a challenge to write down what you are thankful for. I think that what you are thankful for is a personal declaration. If you want to post how you feel, that's fine. Anyway, the purpose is to become more aware of the blessings in your life. What you are grateful for should outweigh the people, places, and things that bring difficulty into your life. For example, you might experience difficulty with someone at work. The good news is that you can turn your negative situations around. It takes time, work, and a grateful heart. Be happy, and happiness will prevail.

February 16

Affirmation: I will work on letting go of my pain and venture out of my comfort zone.

Misery can be comforting. If you start a conversation with how hard life is or how terrible you feel, you might get sympathy. *I have been waiting for you to show up so I can dump my misery at your doorstep. And oh, by the way, don't even think of trying to outdo my lousy circumstances; you won't win.* Have you ever had these thoughts or similar ones? People just love to let others know how hard they have it.

It is vitally important to have friends and loved ones who will listen and be sympathetic to what you are going through. It's the need to share and the need to shock that are vastly different. Many don't want to share their trials and tribulations, sorrows and struggles for that very same reason. It's a fine line between taking advantage of someone and truly being with them and allowing them into what is going on with you. It is a matter of trust—trusting yourself and your feelings and trusting other people in your lives not to judge, criticize, or give you unwarranted advice. It can take a day or many days or even years to develop this kind of relationship, but when you leave this world, may it be with one thing: a close friend nearby.

February 17

Affirmation: Today when I need a break, I will take a break.

"Rest" and "relaxation" are not dirty words. If you are to move at your best pace, think rationally, and treat others with dignity and respect, then you must take the time out of your busy day to take a step back when you are feeling stressed, tired, or overwhelmed. Actually, not only will the people around you benefit, as will you, but they often will be glad that you are taking care of yourself in body, mind, and spirit.

So today, instead of pushing yourself beyond your limits and becoming angry, frustrated, or shut down, acknowledge the moment when you need to take a break, a nap, or simply a breath. Earned rest is the best type of rest.

February 18

Affirmation: Today I will push through my tendency to pull back.

When was the last time you wanted to get away from it all? There is a phenomenon called cocooning, whereby people who are feeling stressed or overwhelmed tend more and more to stay at home and be less involved in clubs, organizations, and other types of functions.

The fact is we are all connected. When feeling overwhelmed, the more we connect with the source of creation—life force, higher power, God, whatever name is most comfortable—the more enlivened, empowered, and energized we become.

Teams, orchestras, clubs, and even politicians can't function in a vacuum. Not only is there strength in numbers, but also the talents and gifts that one person brings are enhanced by what another has to contribute. When you acknowledge a connection, you are in a position to offer less aggression and more compassion, less judgment and more grace, and less apathy and more kindness.

February 19

Affirmation: Today I will start something new without focusing on the outcome.

Are you outcome driven? Painting, singing, dancing, writing, mowing the lawn ... it all starts out with the first attempt being less than perfect. Or perhaps you were lucky and got it right the first time. Perfectionism is a futile goal. Striving to do your best is a much better choice in life.

Talk to anyone who has ever produced anything. They will tell you about their failed attempts. The missed opportunities for some are their most memorable.

What opportunity that you haven't tried and failed is still interesting to you now? Think for a moment about what you liked to do as a child but gave up as you grew older. What did you want to be when you grew up? In your youth, did you dance a lot, play with clay, or like to build things? Did you want to be a firefighter or a teacher? Look deep inside and get in touch with your inner child. What would you tell your ten-year-old self today about missed opportunities? Sing, soar, dance, and have fun. Nobody cares if you succeed or fail. Do what you want to do that will bring you happiness and a sense of accomplishment.

February 20

Affirmation: Today I will be instrumental in helping others to achieve their goals.

A good leader empowers others. A good leader is available, consistent, and fair. If a leader wants others to follow, then he or she must be aware of the needs and wants of the people with whom that leader is working. Have you had a boss who was aggressive and authoritarian? Or have you had a leader who was passive and permissive? This goes for parents and other relationships, as well. The key to any working relationship is assertiveness—that is, getting your needs and wants met without hurting anyone else. Great leaders are those who empower others. What makes a good leader in your book? Are you that person?

February 21

Affirmation: Today I will say what I mean and mean what I say.

Authenticity is when what you say and what you feel are in alignment with what you think. Thinking, saying, feeling, and doing the same things consistently create a balance in your relationships with friends, loved ones, and colleagues. Being clear and consistent is important when living an authentic lifestyle.

It is a conscious decision to maintain balance in your life by not going too far off in one direction, to the detriment of the ones around you. It is when you think and act impulsively that you find yourself not being the person you want to be. How many times have you said, "I wish I could have done that differently"? Well, perhaps you could have. Perhaps you acted a certain way because you thought it was expected of you. You acted in a way that was inconsistent with whom and what you are.

Being out of balance is when what you are currently doing in your life interferes with or negatively impacts your life. When you find yourself in a place that is not representative of your best self, get help. Talk to a friend, family member, clergyperson, or counselor. Turn it around. Once you know better, do better.

February 22

Affirmation: Nobody knows what I do until I don't do it.

Do the right thing even if nobody's going to know whether you did it or not. Do what you are supposed to do even if no one is looking. No one knows what you do until you don't do it. Just think of all the things you do or don't do in a twenty-four–hour period. The age-old question is: do you feel appreciated? If not, look around and notice that you have set it up so that you get what you ask for. That sounds harsh, but you cause your circumstances. Many of us take shortcuts or leave tasks undone in the hopes that someone else will come along and do it for us. *Why do I have to do everything?*

There are thousands of excuses we use to get out of doing whatever it is we don't want to do or we are not in the mood to do. The fact is that you are the one and only person who is responsible for yourself and what you have committed to do, at work, at home, and even in relationships.

We don't have to do everything when we have too much on our plate, but if that is truly the case, ask for help rather than just let things go undone. Teach others to do their share so that they will know firsthand the degree of difficulty and learn responsibility. Teach them that a kind word of thanks goes a long way. Encouragement is key to appreciation.

February 23

Affirmation: Today I will stop and listen when someone I know needs me.

It is very difficult to say that you have control over your own happiness. It's true that if you think and act positively, your mood will improve. That goes without saying. But what happens when you are feeling low, when you find yourself feeling down? The most difficult thing to do when you are in a terrible mood is to "snap out of it." When people point out that you have no apparent reason to feel sad, they feel obligated to tell you to cheer up. There is something called "clinical depression," and approximately fifteen million Americans suffer from major depression that does not easily go away and needs treatment by a doctor and/or a therapist. Do you feel this way or know someone who does?

The good news is there is effective treatment available. Getting help is the hardest step, but it is the first step to feeling better and the only step oftentimes to living a better, happier life. Are you someone who sees the glass half-empty or feels helpless or hopeless? Or, perhaps, you are guilty of telling people that things aren't as bad as they seem. We all need our feelings validated at times . "Someone else may have it worse, so don't be sad," is like saying someone else might have it better, so don't be happy.

February 24

Affirmation: I will treat others how I wish to be treated.

How often do you stop and think, *Maybe I could have been nicer to that person. Perhaps I was wrong and took my anger out on that man.* Being impatient with people, talking about people behind their backs, and being judgmental are ways you treat others but would never want to be treated in return.

Think of how you treat your family members when you are not at your best. Are you overly harsh? Do you take a stand against what they want just to be right? Do you lash out when, in fact, they are innocent and you are the one who is in the wrong?

When you're feeling down or in a position of weakness in your personal life, you may project your unhappiness onto others in the form of treating them badly. Generally, this is an automatic reaction to your stress level and current state of mind. Once you react harshly, you wish you could take it back. When dealing with others, be aware of your current state of mind, how you are feeling. Take a moment to check in with how you are feeling and what you are thinking at that moment prior to interacting with others. It only takes a second, but checking yourself before reacting negatively is important for you and for the person with whom you are with. Stop yourself before you have feelings of remorse.

Notice when you treat others with dignity and respect. Think about the times you are loving and fair to others. Be kind to others, and sit back and witness the kindness coming back to you.

February 25

Affirmation: Today I will breathe deeper and with greater purpose.

Whenever you feel down, remember to start breathing again. Breathing comes naturally. If you are alive, you are continually breathing. So then, why is it that when you are stressed out and overwrought, someone comes up to you and tells you to breathe? Take a breath. "Of course, I'm breathing" is what you say to yourself.

When you are stressed out, breathe deeply and purposefully. You are slowing down and refocusing your mind, body, and spirit. You are putting yourself in a more balanced and, therefore, more relaxed state. At times chaos and pressure prevent you from being aware of your breathing. Of course, you can't be in touch or even aware of your breathing all the time, but you can make a concerted effort to stop at intervals during the day and meditate or simply breathe slowly and with purpose. Be aware of your breath going in slowly, and exhale slowly. Healthy breathing can prevent or diminish anxiety. Breathing properly fills our body with an optimal amount of oxygen, which helps relieve stress and increases our concentration capacity. Proper breathing can be learned or improved with daily breathing exercises.

February 26

Affirmation: You never know what someone has been through. Today I won't judge on looks.

The reason people have pretty smiles, pretty eyes, and kind hearts is that they allow themselves to cry the tears and feel the pain. Sometimes the prettiest smiles hide the deepest secrets. The prettiest eyes have cried more tears. And the kindest hearts have felt the most pain.

Forgiveness and acceptance are the best beauty secrets. Deal with your sorrow, and then do what you have to do to move on. Those of us who do not keep our feelings in release the stress and anxiety that are toxic. If you want to feel beautiful and look amazing, try letting go of whatever it is that is bothering you. Love life, and give love to others. Share your experiences, good or bad. Learn and grow into the beautiful person you are meant to be.

February 27

Affirmation: I don't worry. It's a waste of time.

Worrying stops you from enjoying the goodness of life. Worrying doesn't stop bad things from happening. Worrying is a learned behavior. Are you a worrier?

Worrying is an emotion that is learned from someone in your life. Who taught you how to worry? Your mom, your dad, a grandparent, or another family member might be responsible for teaching you how to worry through his or her words and actions. The thing about worrying is that it is a total waste of time and energy and serves absolutely no purpose. You were not born to worry. Refusing to worry will absolutely improve your quality of life. No one tells you that everything will be better if you just worry a little more. How then can you get yourself to stop worrying?

Worrying is simply a bad habit, and, like any bad habit, you have to want to stop. You must first come to the realization that worrying does absolutely no good and that time and energy can be spent in better, healthier, and more helpful ways. Then you have to become aware of the times you find yourself worrying and what it is that you worry about. Let it go. Have faith that everything will work out just fine. The opposite of worry is faith. Have faith in yourself and others. Have faith that no matter what happens, it will work out. The fact is that tragedy and pain and suffering are a part of life. Worrying about them will never prevent pain and sorrow. Deal with the negative when it presents itself. Don't bring it on sooner by thinking the worse.

February 28

Affirmation: The opposite of worry is faith ... faith in all outcomes for the enrichment and enhancement of goodness.

Faith knows that all will be well within your heart, soul, and mind if you can let go of control and worry. Faith is a knowing in your heart what cannot easily be explained or proven. When you worry, you are reacting to the need to control things and the people in your life. You need to have things a certain way, your way, and you aren't able or willing to leave anything to chance. When you worry, you live your life out of fear. You fear that the worst will happen if you are not there to see that it doesn't, and when things go wrong you blame yourself for not being there to change the outcome. This is mental cruelty. If this sounds familiar to you and you are a worrier, or perhaps someone you know is, give faith a chance—faith that the world will go on, as it should, that you are not in control of everything; in fact, you are in control of very little. Take a moment to trust in others and yourself to be able to handle what lies ahead.

February 29
Leap Year

Affirmation: Today I will take a leap of faith.

If you were born on February 29, you may be keenly aware that this is an intercalary day that comes only once every four years. Intercalary, for those of you who don't know (I certainly didn't) is a day inserted in the calendar to harmonize it with the solar year. The reason for 366 days, every four years, is to maintain synchronicity with the astronomical or seasonal year. Synchronicity and harmony combined. They say this day brings forth those chosen few.

Whether today is your birthday, or not, take a chance today. Take a leap of faith. A leap of faith refers to believing in something, someone, or even yourself without knowing for certain what is going to happen next. Creative and passionate endeavors require us to start fresh with unbridled abandon. Today, be open to the possibilities of what lies ahead. Assess the risks and then, one step at a time, let your spirit soar.

March

National Nutrition Month

March 1

Affirmation: I don't need approval from others. I am self-reliant. I think for myself.

Have you figured out yet that what other people think of you doesn't matter? I know this for sure. People have their own biased opinions, and they may or may not agree with you. When it comes to your life, other people can be wrong.

Children need guidance. We all need help with a multitude of situations in our lives. Guidance is necessary and often crucial. Needing or requiring other people's approval or caring what other people think of you, however, is not healthy.

Allowing others, even loved ones, to rob you of your thoughts, ideas, and ability to make decisions takes away the one thing that makes you who you are. Your uniqueness and your individuality come from asserting yourself, right or wrong. Make decisions about your life that come from your needs, wants, and priorities. Your thoughts are yours. Trust yourself. You can do this. Know yourself, and think for yourself. What do you think of that?

March 2

Affirmation: Dysfunction is not healthy.

We hear the word *dysfunctional* every day: dysfunctional family, dysfunctional relationships, and even erectile dysfunction.

Dysfunction is abnormal behavior. It refers to behavior that is out of whack and not working. Dysfunction occurs when someone is plagued with conflict and misbehavior. Behaviorally, unhealthy people are dysfunctional role models. They are generally unaware of what they're doing wrong.

Dysfunction tends to be the norm in some families, and it has the potential to spill over to future generations. We see it on reality shows all the time. The drama is compelling. These people act badly. They look to others to blame for their negative behavior. They point fingers and never see their role in the breakdown of a quality life. They're seemingly happy in their ignorance. It appears that either they don't know any better or they don't care. Change may be too difficult. Perhaps they give up trying.

How do you get out of a dysfunctional rut? Start each day by doing what it takes to improve your life or better your circumstances in a meaningful way, one that works for your benefit and those around you. Your future starts with you.

March 3

Affirmation: Today I will get out of my head.
Too much thinking is not good for me.

Thinking is painful for most people. Overthinking about the past or the future is often extremely unproductive. Having constant chatter in your head is anxiety producing and causes worry. "What if" thinking will drive you crazy. Thinking too much can lead to doubt and insecurity. Relax. Have faith.

Talk it out. Meditate. Rest. Quiet your mind. Sometimes the more you think, the less you know. Sometimes it is helpful to remind yourself to just be.

March 4

Affirmation: How people treat you is their karma; how you react is yours.

I never dispute the spiritual principle of karma. What comes around goes around. How you act is how you are treated. Karma is also the Golden Rule. Treat other people, as you would have them treat you.

Why then is it so hard to be nice all the time? You want and even expect others to be nice to you. You never walk into a situation thinking that the person behind the counter is going to be mean and nasty to you. But you know for sure that if you are mean and nasty, mean and nasty are what you're going to get back. Is it safe to say that you treat people with dignity and respect most of the time? The irony is that we sometimes tend to not be very nice enough to our loved ones and those closest to us.

Now would be a good time to stop taking your problems out on others. Enjoy the way others will respond to the new you.

March 5

Affirmation: Today when I need a break I will take a break.

Let's get down to taking care of the "stuff in your head." Unresolved issues that plague you wreak havoc on your physical and mental health. Suppressing or repressing whatever it is that you are not dealing with can be dangerous. If you are thinking too much and are unable or unwilling to let go, you also may feel unproductive, stuck, or even ill.

Walk away for a minute or two from whatever it is that's bothering you. Change your situation, and gather your thoughts in a healthy way. It's virtually always healing to walk away and then come back refreshed and ready to handle whatever presents itself to you.

Decide what is best for you, trust yourself, and move on. Talk it out with a friend. Research shows the importance of writing in a journal when overwhelmed. Meditate and pray. Let it go, and quiet your mind. Your health is worth it!

March 6

Affirmation: Today I will call on my insight to overcome adversity.

A *lightbulb moment* is a moment of sudden inspiration, revelation, or recognition. It has the power to affirm your brilliance. What is considered a *lightbulb moment* comes when the feeling of a "burst of light" illuminates what is happening with you at that particular moment. It's when the light comes on and you see things clearly. At that moment everything is in sync and you know exactly what it is you need to know. It's telling you that the answer is right in front of you. You are amazing. Be inspired. Be inspiring. Shine your light.

March 7

Affirmation: The perfect prayer is "Please and thank you."

We teach our children at a very young age always to have good manners. We teach them to say, "Please," and "Thank you." But are we really teaching them the importance of giving thanks and having a grateful heart? It's a concept that is necessary and hopefully learned sometime in your life. "Please give me strength." "Thank you for all of my blessings." "Please help my loved one, my friend, or my neighbor."

When you're grateful and begin the day with a thankful heart, the worries of the day can seem insignificant. When you're grateful and give thanks, you have the power to spread good feelings to your part of the world. When you recognize how you've been blessed, give a prayer of thanks. It is so simple yet so powerful.

March 8

Affirmation: Today I will pause when I need to.

HALT is an acronym for "Don't be too *hungry*, *angry*, *lonely*, or *tired*." It is when a moment is needed before reacting badly to any given situation. This is true for children, as well as adults. When you are angry, think about what is behind the feeling. We often are not mad at the person (or circumstance) at whom we think we are mad. Balance is stopping to be certain your needs are taken care of first and foremost.

Take a look at what is going on with you in the moment when you are not being your best self. To some, happiness comes easily. Perhaps you were just born that way. For others, it is a struggle to be happy. You start out thinking that the day is going to go your way, and then life happens. Perhaps you feel that other people have it easier, but we all experience bumps in the road from time to time. The difference between you and some other person is how you deal with adversity, how you respond to things not going your way. Are you angry in traffic? Are you easily frustrated when you are seemingly not in control? What do you do to get out of the negative and into a more positive way of handling the situation? Start with a greater awareness of HALT, and see if you don't feel better.

March 9

Affirmation: Awareness begs responsibility.

Once you know what needs to be done to make positive changes in your life, you have to take the necessary steps to bring about those changes. It sounds simple, right? Once you are on your way, you'll need to make the appropriate changes an integral part of your life. Now is the time to start.

Accepting that change is inevitable is huge. Becoming aware of what needs to change in your life is crucial. In some situations you might be the last to know change is imminent. You might be the last to know that what you're doing is no longer working.

Whether it's your personal or professional life that requires change, acceptance is the key. You must accept the fact that your past choices are no longer healthy and that a brighter future is ahead for you and your loved ones.

Write down the behavior(s) you want to change. Note what you are doing at the time and whom you are with. How are you feeling? Whether it is getting into shape or wanting to be more attentive to your partner's needs, it's necessary to detect a pattern. Once you know more about the behavior you want to change, it's time to let go. Substitute healthier choices, make certain that you are prepared, and have the tools necessary for the adjustment period. Enlist a friend or someone who is going through what you are and is motivated to change too. Don't give up until you've made the change. Don't stop until the negative behavior you are working on changing is a thing of the past.

March 10

Affirmation: When I think I can't go on, I remember I know I can, and then I do.

Running a 5K, distance swimming, and even reading and writing are individual sports. Whatever it is you take on, more often than not, you have to ultimately do it on your own.

The good news is that you get the good feelings of accomplishment and achievement afterward. When you start out, you're filled with energy and enthusiasm. You've been looking forward to this for a while. You get what you need, you're all set to go, the process starts, and then you find yourself wanting to quit the moment you start. A little voice inside your head says, "What am I thinking? I can't do that!" You want to run in the opposite direction. "No one will care if I quit."

It's at this very crucial moment that it's imperative to let go of any inhibitions and silence your inner critic. Allow your inner strength and fortitude to rev up. *I think I can, and I know I can.* Stay strong, and stay positive. The power of affirmation is exactly what you need to get the job done. There comes a point when you realize you can only do your best, and your best is going to have to be good enough. Before long you are getting into the swing of things and no longer want to turn around. Go for it. It'll all be worth it. Trust yourself. You've got this!

March 11

Affirmation: Happiness is living life as it should be, as it is meant to be.

When you love someone, his or her happiness matters. That person's health and well-being are important for you to be happy. If someone you love is sick, unhappy, or miserable, you hurt also. You think of things that you can do to make that person's life better. You give advice, cook a meal, or bring gifts. You do whatever you think you need to do to ease his or her pain.

When the fog is lifted on that person's misery, you breathe a sigh of relief and shout for joy. All is well, and all is as it should be. But what about when making someone else happy is out of your control? You can only offer your kindness and support. Only the person who is hurting can change his or her circumstances. Now what? All you can do is be patient. Don't give up on your loved one. Try to be there for that person when he or she is ready. Love is compassionate. Love accepts people as they are. Love endures all and believes all. I know there will come a time when you have those moments of pure joy. Be happy, be healthy, and take care of those you love.

If the person in your life is abusive in any way, the love you give him or her is no longer enough. You may find yourself enabling that person's negativity. Seek help to restore yourself emotionally. It may be necessary to take a step back and walk away.

March 12

Affirmation: Today I will choose not to suffer.

Suffering is not accepting or understanding life. When we love someone, we open ourselves up to joy, happiness, pain, and suffering. We also open ourselves up to loving feelings that words cannot describe. We may, at times, hurt the ones we love, even though they are always there for us, just as we try to be there for them.

What's all the pain and suffering about? They happen when you see your loved ones in trouble and hurting. You suffer when you don't understand or accept what they're going through or exactly what they're doing. You suffer when what they have to give is not what you want or need at the time. Don't lose hope.

Recognize the people in your life that are worth suffering for. Everyone you love is going to hurt (not abuse) you at some time or another, because to love is to feel pain and loss. Celebrate the people in your life who minimize your pain and suffering, and, in doing so, find your joy.

March 13

Affirmation: Today I will choose to accept myself as I am.

Acceptance is acknowledging the facts of the situation and then recognizing what you need to do next. Accepting yourself for whom and what you are is not easy. Sometimes it's easier to be hard on yourself and be self-critical.

Perhaps you're unhappy with your physical appearance. It's easy to think of yourself as less than beautiful when looking at magazine models with touched-up bodies. You can think of only how great they look and how you pale in comparison. Perhaps you are not where you want to be in your life and would rather be doing something more exciting. You feel as if you can't catch a break, as if nothing ever goes right for you. Or perhaps you dwell on what was and compare yourself to a younger version of yourself. Perhaps you are reluctant to accept your circumstances or what's happened to you so far in life and can't move on. The past can be crippling for many.

Once you accept what it is you are all about in life—your purpose and your reason for living—you can keep what's worth keeping and let go of the rest. What are you going to do about what you're not happy with in your life? It's a choice. Your life decisions are your choices to make.

March 14

Affirmation: Today I will accept my life the way it is.

We all experience trouble in our lives when nothing is as it should be. When hard times come, it is difficult at best to be positive about anything in life. We all have days that turn into months when we are broken and it is extremely difficult to turn it around. (If this is not the case for you perhaps you know or love someone who is currently going through a rough patch.)

We cannot change anything in life until we accept it, first and foremost. Accept the problem areas with the people, places, and things in your life. Accept the things over which you have no control. If you can make adjustments in your life be open to solicit help from others. Perhaps you can be instrumental in making life easier for someone else. Ease your burden by lifting someone else up. Do it with love, kindness, and understanding. Do it with care and concern. You just might find that you have the courage to handle what you are currently facing. Accept that this is what we are called to do. Acceptance is a wonderful thing.

March 15

Affirmation: I am a good friend.

There are people who have lots of friends and acquaintances. There are those who have a small, intimate circle of close friends. There are folks who have one or two amazing friends, and that's all they need.

The gift of making friends is a blessing. It's being joyful and loving while sharing your time, talents, and companionship with others. Staying friends with others is not easy over time. You have to put forth the effort to stay in touch, stay informed, and be there in good times and in bad. Above all, you must be a friend who can be trusted. Good friends are nonjudgmental and have the ability to listen when needed. Almost everyone, at one time or another, has walked away from a friendship. That's never easy, but sometimes it's necessary.

Friends care about you and laugh with you. They make you feel heard and understood. Friends are there through whatever life throws at you. Reach out to someone today. You never know when you'll need someone in your corner. Being able to make friends is a blessing.

March 16

Affirmation: Happiness is singing your own song and dancing to your own beat.

Live your life your way no matter what anyone says. Does it really matter when you're in the shower or driving in the car if you have a good singing voice or not? Some people are blessed and can sing well. Some of you may be great singers. What is it about singing that is so universal? Singing is a release. You can let it all out.

Let go of the stored emotions of the day. Allow yourself simply to breathe and to get in touch with the emotions of your soul. When you're sad, listening to a sad song can be amazing. It allows you to feel as if you're not the only one suffering. Or, to the contrary, when you are sad, listening to upbeat music can lift your spirits. When you're happy and sing along to a familiar song, your heart soars.

Singing and dancing on the most basic level can lift your mood and put you in a better place. Music propels you to be more productive and more responsive to yourself and others. The most amazing song you can possibly sing is a song to a child. Try dancing with someone who never dances. Do your own thing, sing, and dance as much as possible.

March 17

Affirmation: Today I will dance.

Singing, dancing, and laughing are fun. Playfulness is restorative and good for the soul. Letting go and having fun are healthy to mind, body, and spirit. Singing and dancing are artful forms of expression. When you're alone, turn up the music and dance or sing your heart out. There are those who have been dancing or singing all their life, and it is their passion. There are those who never got a chance to dance or sing. Maybe you downright refuse to get on the dance floor. People plead and beg, but you're not budging. You're not giving in, no way, no how.

What the dancers of the world know for sure is that you're missing out on all the fun. The reason you don't dance is that the last time you attempted to get out on the dance floor it wasn't pretty or you felt embarrassed and self-conscious. Maybe you're afraid. We've all been there. What is different about those who dance and those who don't is that the joy of dancing wins out over the embarrassment every time. Dancing is good for the soul, and it makes people happy. It doesn't get better than that.

March 18

Affirmation: I think I can.

At times it's easy to psych yourself out. The problem is that too often you talk yourself out of doing something that's good for you. If you can talk yourself out of doing something that's good for you, you can certainly talk yourself out of doing something that's bad for you. Naturally. What is it that you want to start doing or stop doing?

I want to start doing__________________________.
I want to stop doing___________________________.

You can change the behaviors you listed simultaneously, but it might be better to tackle one thing at a time, one day at a time. Change does not happen overnight. It takes consistency and dedication on your part. Pick a habit you want to quit, and replace it with a healthier alternative. Start something that will make you happy, and keep it up. No one has to tell you what you need to work on. You know your strengths and weaknesses. You also know what to do. You know better than anyone else.

March 19

Affirmation: Today I will look to a young person for insight and inspiration.

Grow old to be young again. Far too many people take themselves too seriously. Have you played with a Frisbee lately? When was the last time you blew bubbles with no children around? Next time you are at the market, buy yourself a soccer ball, a tennis ball, or a large inflatable beach ball. Now go have fun. I know you know what to do.

As young children we are taught to act our age. Growing up was a journey that was exciting and thrilling but took forever. Each milestone was a giant leap into a new stage of life—new responsibilities, new questions, and new rules to the game. When we are children, we want to be teenagers. When we are teenagers, we want to be adults.

At what point does the vision of your life's journey turn into looking back over your shoulder rather than looking ahead to a bright future? Maybe you think that the future doesn't appear to be promising and the past looks a whole lot better. This can be a normal progression of aging. When you realize that the past is gone and the only choice you have is to make a better future is when happiness shows up. Each birthday is a chance to reflect and go into the next year, the next stage of life, with dignity and eyes wide open.

March 20

International Day of Happiness

Affirmation: Today I choose happiness and reject misery.

It might be easy for someone with a sunny disposition to be happy all the time. When people are angry or unhappy, the optimist is uncomfortable and doesn't understand why. He or she doesn't understand why grumpy people can't see the glass half-full. On the other hand, someone who is negative all the time (the pessimist) doesn't understand the happy-go-lucky optimist. Let's not forget the realists and idealists.

For some it can be a defense mechanism to be happy all the time. The optimist doesn't want to be unhappy at all costs. Others are used to being in a perpetual lousy mood and become accustomed to it. They feel they have a reason to be mad and don't care if others like it or not. Pessimists may think happiness is overrated.

You probably fall somewhere in the middle. It's hard to maintain happiness, and it's difficult to get out of a bad mood. With reality shows and media constantly promoting negativity, senseless fighting, and constant bickering, we're bombarded with bad behavior leaving everyone feeling bad or down. Perhaps the culture promotes misery.

Either you can give yourself permission to be balanced in body, mind, and spirit or you can allow yourself to be defeated. It's up to you. Happiness is an attitude; it is a choice.

March 21

Affirmation: Today I will lighten up.

Taking yourself too seriously can be problematic. What it says about people is that they think they must say certain things or act a certain way that it is beneath them to let their hair down. What will people think? Perhaps you were praised for being this way as a child and reprimanded for "cutting up."

When you take life too seriously, you must be highly diligent in all areas of your life. You think if you let go, you'll fall. It matters to you if you're not always doing what needs to be done.

No one ever looked back on life and said, "I should have been more serious." Life is full of sorrow and joy. A proper blend of seriousness and lighthearted humor is the perfect balance. Look for an opportunity today to take time to laugh and seriously enjoy life.

March 22

Affirmation: I am amazing.

When you're exceptional at what you do, people are taken aback. Why? Because when someone excels, it's a beautiful thing. The person is wholly dedicated to a skill and has created beauty.

In an environment where excellence is expected, the bar is set very high. Reaching (or exceeding) expectations is an amazing accomplishment and provides a tremendous feeling. However, life is not a competition. It's not a race. Life is about setting goals and actualizing your own personal best. It's about taking your passion to the next level. Continue onward and upward. You have the desire, and you have the vision.

Some people aren't used to excellence and quality being expected of them. If this is the case for you, set your own standards, and raise the bar slightly higher than you think is obtainable. We can all do better, and we can all reach higher. Having faith in yourself and your abilities is the key. You are capable and competent.

March 23

Affirmation: Today I will pitch in and make a difference.

Everybody must get involved to improve the quality of the environment. When people are environmentally responsible, commend them. The best way to keep the planet healthy and protected is by setting an example yourself. If others see you throwing your plastics in the recycling bin, perhaps they will do the same thing. Maybe your town's waste disposal program needs improvement or your contractor uses unsafe chemicals. Speaking up is proactive.

Volunteer at a program that teaches young children about how to be good stewards of the planet. Earth Day was designed for just that reason. Educate yourself and others on what can be done to make the earth safe for future generations. You know what to do, so do what you can. Being good to the earth is guaranteed to make you feel better. Feel better, and get well soon. Mother Earth is counting on you.

March 24

Affirmation: Loving the earth is prayer.

Never being alone sounds too good to be true. How often do you feel that your life is mundane, boring, or monotonous? Go outside and really experience nature, as often as possible. Take a hike. Go river rafting. Ride your bicycle. Plant a garden. Walk your dog. The air, trees, wind, and rivers are rejuvenating. The forces of nature are mysterious and invite you to stop and think of what exactly your purpose in life is. Have you gotten complacent, where one day turns into the next? Ski a mountain, ice-skate, or make a snow angel. Surf, go swimming, or simply sit under an oak tree.

It's all for the same good. Nature is yours for its beauty and magnitude. Trees give us purpose and life. Water gives us pause to appreciate the vastness in contrast to our tiny speck of existence on planet earth. The sky houses life and endless beauty. When you are down, go for a walk, look around you, and, as you wander, ponder. The beauty and mysteries of life are here to keep us company and to remind us that we are never alone.

March 25

Affirmation: You always know.

“You always know” is a life-affirming statement. People reply “I don’t know” way too often and out of habit. When you say you don’t know, you are saying that you don’t want to say what’s on your mind. “I don’t know” translates to “I’m not going to take responsibility for my answer.” What you’re saying in essence is “I don’t know if I want to answer you.”

Perhaps you are caught off guard and haven’t had time to think of your response. Perhaps you are afraid of being judged or criticized.

The next time someone asks for your opinion, think about what is being asked of you and take a moment to think of your response. What is being asked of you is probably not as earth-shattering as you might think. Will your response rock the world? Will what you have to say be scrutinized or, worse, used against you? In most cases, I don’t think so. The person with whom you’re talking is asking for your thoughts for a reason—possibly to shed some light on a confusing situation or perhaps to have his or her way of thinking validated by someone he or she trusts. When someone is engaging you in conversation and asks you a question, it’s either to enlist your opinion or to include you in a friendly exchange. It’s okay to speak up and speak your mind, as long as you are not hurting anyone. Try it. Take “I don’t know” out of your vocabulary. What others think of you is not as important as you think. Be confident and speak your truth

March 26

Affirmation: Change is good.

Life is a gift. Each day brings new opportunities and new circumstances to make the best of your situation and work with what you have, not with what you wish you had. How is that accomplished? By not only thinking positively but by having specific, original, and unique thoughts. By being thankful and coming from a place of gratitude. We don't get what we want all the time.

You have a chance each and every day to take the circumstances of your life and change your way of thinking. Think about things in a different light. Perhaps those closest to you have been telling you the same thing over and over for years and you're not listening. Try looking at your situation from a different perspective. Let go of your fears and apprehension, and try a new approach. Perhaps a different way of looking at things might be right for you after all.

Design your life the way you want it to be. Make changes if necessary, and never settle for less. You can live the life you want and be happy or settle for an uninspiring, unfulfilling existence. It's up to you. Take that leap of faith, and go back to school. Change jobs if that's what you want, or even change your career. Reassess the people with whom you associate. Whom you are with is vital to a fulfilled life. Are there relationships in your life that need mending? Think about the toxic people in your life who prevent you from being happy. Reevaluate your relationships, and be with people because you genuinely want to, not because you think you have to.

Think about the future with eyes wide open. See it through your own eyes as beautiful brushstrokes of color. Think of where you want to be, what you want to be doing, and with whom you want to do it. Be thankful for your ability and the opportunity to change. Let go of all bad thoughts, and create new, more positive ones.

March 27

Affirmation: My life has purpose and significance.

Achieving happiness in life is what matters most. How do you obtain happiness? Happiness equals peace. Therefore, to obtain happiness, you must rid yourself (if possible) of all that is not working in your life and all that is causing you stress. Do what you love to do. Find your passion, and determine how you can dedicate your life to that pursuit. Let go of what is not needed or wanted in your life.

Take time to enjoy your life. Have fun with whatever it is that you enjoy. Get back into activities that you have perhaps stopped doing.

Chances are you have let go of things you enjoy, because you told yourself you don't have time for them anymore. Hopefully, that could not be further from the truth. Allowing leisure time for games, activities, sports, and music is what completes us and makes us happy. When you pursue a pastime that brings you peace, it is easier to be stress-free and relaxed. Having fun is highly beneficial. It prevents the stress of work, family, daily living, and so on from overcoming and overwhelming you.

March 28

Affirmation: Today I will radiate peace within me. I will smile.

With just a smile you can bring happiness and joy to people who are perhaps in an otherwise miserable situation. Remember—when you smile for no apparent reason, people wonder what you're up to.

Give a smile away today. When you smile at someone, that person might pause for a second and then hopefully smile back. This may be the only ray of sunshine that person receives today.

Mother Teresa brought hope and love to the poorest of the poor with a smile in her heart. Your trials and tribulations may pale in comparison. Go through life with a smile on your face and peace in your heart.

March 29

Affirmation: Today I will do something positive for the environment.

Your home reflects your attitude and expectations. So it is with the world in which you live. Are you complacent, and do you just not care? Or are you meticulous, and must you have everything just right? Most of us fall somewhere in the middle. You want a clean environment, one in which things are as they should be. You want your surroundings to be comfortable and inviting. You don't want your home, garden, or workplace to be dirty and nasty.

What do you have to do to honor your living space and the earth you call home? It's not that difficult. When you see something on the ground, pick it up. When you have trash, recycle it. Stop using plastic water bottles, and stop eating foods wrapped in plastic. Use hand dryers instead of paper. Google the many things you can do personally to help clean up your world.

As far as your living space is concerned, keeping it clean and comfortable makes your life stress-free and relaxed. Keeping up with household chores provides a haven for you and your family to enjoy your time together without fighting over who is going to do what. When it comes to household chores, clarity, commitment, and consistency are not bad things.

March 30

Affirmation: I will put others' needs and wants ahead of my own, just for today.

Thinking about and caring for the welfare of others are transforming. When you decide to give of your time and talent to others, you receive self-fulfilled joy immediately.

When you give of yourself to another human being, you are spreading love, kindness, joy, and understanding. You are giving hope to someone who might have given up. You perhaps are providing someone with the most basic necessities in life. You are perhaps getting away from your misery when faced with someone who has it far worse than you. Giving of your time and talent is always a positive activity.

Perhaps you don't know where to begin. Maybe you don't trust that your support gets to those who need it most. It doesn't matter if you initially have faith in the process or not. When you begin to think about how you can help others, help is what happens—not just in the life of others but in your life, as well.

March 31

Affirmation: Today I will ponder my dreams and do what it takes to make them a reality.

The beauty of life is the secret to happiness. Beauty in all forms makes us better. Why do you think there is beauty all around you? The sky, sea, and flowers have amazing color and light for our enjoyment. Birds, ladybugs, and bunny rabbits all bring joy to those who stop to watch and observe. When you are feeling sluggish or tired, walk outside and feel the sun, the rain, or the wind on your face; then go back to what you were doing, and be rejuvenated.

Noticing what is right in front of you is living your life abundantly and with purpose. Be aware of what is healthy and available to you. Be open to the possibility of enjoying life and living it to the fullest.

You can't live a healthy, purposeful life if you are not paying attention. What excites you? When was the last time you felt awed? Go there. Just go there.

April

Stress Awareness Month

April 1

Affirmation: Today I will think before I speak.

In this fast-paced world in which we live, people say things like "If I don't get my thought out now, I'll forget it." The art of conversation is lost. People talk or text on their cell phones and are preoccupied with a dozen different mediums other than the art of true communication between people in the here and now. Some people text the person who is sitting across the table from them! What impact does this have on relationships and interpersonal communication? It's potentially a ticking time bomb. Don't get me wrong. How many times have you witnessed a family out to dinner when the mom, dad, and children are all on their cell phones? Some say this keeps the peace, but to what end? Do we really know how to converse anymore, how to debate, how to get our points across?

Is it true? For the most part we are not in the business of lying, but when we talk about others, truthfulness may not be the most important outcome of the story. Sensationalism and shock are the goals of most gossip situations. Is it helpful? You might think people don't want your help. If you can't be helpful, do no harm. Is what you're thinking, feeling, and doing inspiring, necessary, and kind? Saying things like "I don't care what you think, I'm going to tell you how I feel" is just hurtful and wrong. You're much better off keeping it to yourself when your words are not in anyone's best interest or, in fact, are mean. Think before you speak, and think before you act. Now that can't be too hard, can it?

April 2

Affirmation: From where I come is where I'm going.

Why is it that traveling to your destinations seems to take much longer than the ride home? When you arrive home, are you sad for a moment to no longer be away? Or upon returning, do you find comfort in the fact that you are safe and sound, knowing that you are needed? You appreciate that you are part of a whole and part of a family. You're part of a workforce destined to do good things. You're part of a community and a neighborhood of friends. You share a collective purpose. Getting away can be a pleasant escape—no phones, no mail, and no one wanting your undivided attention. *Oh, to live on an island forever.* Doesn't everyone long to be carefree?

April 3

Affirmation: I have what it takes to do the job.

Never give up on your desires, hopes, and dreams. They come to you for a reason. We are inspired by what is presented to us, in the form of a brighter future, because our loving intentions are God inspired. Positive intentions are inspired by our ability to be kind, just, and loving. What comes to us in body, mind, and spirit, in the form of wants and desires, is achievable. How do I know this? Your inner being, your inner soul does not bring forth that which is unobtainable. What you are yearning for to improve yourself or your place in life is God inspired. Pray or meditate on what your next step for goodness might be.

We dream of that which makes us happy, that which brings pure joy and contentment. Many people lose sight of their dreams and give up, lose hope, or quit for a variety of reasons. Perhaps the timing wasn't right. Timing or a lack of money might stand in your way; however, it's never too late to revisit your dreams or develop new ones. Go for it. With hard work, determination, and grace, you can get started on your journey.

April 4

Affirmation: I am where I say I'm going to be.

When you are self-conscious, nervous, anxious, or troubled, the hardest thing to do is to show up. Go to that party, call that friend, or start that new class. You think no one will miss you. The exact opposite is true. A good example is going to worship services. You might not want to, but once you're there, you might just come away feeling stronger and better. The same is true with just about anything you don't really want to do. While you're at it, take into consideration the feelings of the person who invited you and how much your presence means to that person's life. He or she is looking forward to being with you, or he or she wouldn't have asked you in the first place. When you don't show up, you let down yourself and those who love you. So go anyway. Show up when it isn't easy. Show up and have fun.

April 5

Affirmation: I am open to adjusting the way I look at something.

When we are in the throes of anxiety or depression, we truly cannot see the forest for the trees. We continue the same negative behaviors over and over and expect different results. The end result of negative behavior is anger, resentment, loss, and misery. If we are able to seek help and truly acknowledge our part in our own lives and change the negativity, we can then look to the future with kindness and understanding, knowing that we are, in fact, healing. We are now able to move on and be a better version of ourselves.

How you think is how you feel and how you act. When you are not feeling well emotionally, change how you think about the situation. Try to get out of your negativity by changing your surroundings—get out of the house or office, seek out someone who needs your help or someone who can cheer you on. Don't take yourself too seriously. Get through one day at a time rather than seeing down the road with a gloomy outlook. Get out of your own way, and let grace and healing in.

April 6

Affirmation: My faith is strong. I hope for the best.

There are common threads that believing in joy brings. Whether or not you believe in a power greater than yourself (what is commonly known as God or Spirit), hope springs eternal. Hope and faith foster joy—hope in a brighter tomorrow, hope in a relationship turning around, hope in the future, and hope in each other. It all brings a serenity that cannot be denied. Lack of hope is fear. The opposite of hope is discouragement. Negativity can bring only sadness. Without hope and desire, happiness is hard to come by.

Faith is highly subjective; it is highly personalized. Your faith is yours alone. When you come to know what is true in your life, and you've developed, or are working on developing, your own personal belief system, the only proof that you have that you're on the right path is how pure and wonderful those beliefs make you feel.

Do you have clarity with your faith? Does it make sense to you? Does it ring true for you, and does the message of hope and love speak to you? Does having these beliefs make you a better version of yourself? Does your faith make you feel whole? If all this is true and your life is easier, having made the connection to your spirituality, then you are truly on a path to enlightenment. You are truly blessed.

Love is a feeling and a very powerful expression of happiness. The power of love cannot be denied. Find faith in all your experiences. If your struggle with or doubt your faith, seek out what is right for you. Ask questions. Seek counsel. If you lack hope, surround yourself with others who will lift you up. Surround yourself with hopeful people and hopeful situations.

April 7

Affirmation: I will tell myself to take care of my health.

When the body is in good health it is easier to think and act with greater clarity. You are successful in life. Did you know that your mental health is also dependent upon how much exercise and proper nutrition you allow yourself? When you are not in your best shape physically, it is a direct result of what you tell yourself mentally. It is called your internal dialogue. *One more cookie won't hurt. It doesn't matter if I skip the gym today, I'll go tomorrow.* One tomorrow turns into many tomorrows and before you know it you have gotten off track and are no longer motivated to continue your health and wellness plan. The key to maintaining good physical and mental health is to set manageable goals and stay on course. If you are having a lousy day, recognize it as such and get right back on track the very next day. Do not procrastinate! You can go online and find hundreds of Apps that help with eating properly and exercising. Make a concerted effort to educate yourself and work smarter to be healthy. Make it a priority. Set an example for your friends and family. Show them you have what it takes, because you do!

April 8

Affirmation: Today I will leave my comfort zone and be still.

To clear your mind, take a walk. Do you go to your local park often? When you're outside, problems can slip away and your spirit becomes open to clarity. Your heart is open to suggestion when you leave what is predictable and get a change of scenery. Stress is lifted for the moment, thereby giving you a chance to listen to the answers you might need to hear.

When you were a child, you played in the sun and the sand. Children are innocent. As an adult you must get in touch with that purity to make sound decisions. Take a moment to breathe the fresh air and smell the flowers and trees. A nature time-out is needed much more often than you might think.

Daily meditation is the simplest way to find clarity in your thoughts and actions. Meditating outdoors under a lovely tree or beside a river can do wonders for your spirit. Rivers and trees can be found even if you live in a city. Go to a place where there is no sound, turn off your cell phone, and be still. Comfort will come to you.

April 9

Affirmation: Believe in people before they are successful.

I talked with a young lady whose mother does not take her acting aspirations seriously. It turns out that the mother was an actor in college! Why do we not encourage those around us to follow their bliss? Why is it so hard for us to allow the people in our lives not only to succeed but also to become amazing? I believe it's rooted in fear, pure and simple.

When you make a decision that doesn't turn out right for you, it's easy to internalize it as a mistake, when actually making decisions that don't work out can be a good thing. What you do with your life is dependent on your own very unique set of circumstances. Who are you in this moment, physically, mentally, and emotionally?

When advice is needed and you are called upon to help, guide but be careful not to force your values or opinions on anyone else. Check with them; don't assume. Be a cheerleader for those in your life no matter what you think about their life choices or decisions. If you see a young person who wants to sing, dance, or act, give encouragement and praise. It's in their best interest, but it's in yours too.

April 10

Affirmation: I will fail well.

What are your true passions and desires? Do you find that people, circumstances, time, and money have gotten in the way of following your dreams, keeping you from listening to your heart's desire, and letting go of the desire to pursue what you wanted to be when you grew up? Did you want to play an instrument, write, or paint? Did you want to do all those things but felt overwhelmed and gave up? What is holding you back now? Look around. God has given you the dream and will show up to give you what you need to reach your goals if you have the desire, passion, and courage. Courage equals faith. Every great dream begins with a dreamer. Always remember that you have within you the strength, patience, and passion to reach for the stars to change your world.

Find your true passion. Get in touch with that part of yourself that has yet to be discovered and nurtured. Go to the art store, and get a box of pastels. Call up the local community college, and take a course in psychology or business. Sign up for a dance class at a nearby studio. Go for it!

April 11

Affirmation: Today I will think, then I will feel, and then I will act.

There apparently is a trend now that sends the following message: "Say whatever is on you mind" or "I tell it like it is, and too bad if you don't like it." A common response is "What were you thinking?" These statements are highly charged with blatant disregard for the consequences of being brutally honest. Whoever is angered, hurt, or embarrassed is inconsequential. Reality TV tells us to shoot from the hip and then let the other person deal with it, because, after all, life is a competition.

Well, not all of us live on a tropical island, struggling to be the "survivor." In reality, this type of behavior is rude and wrong. Many people don't think before they speak, and it is a detriment to good and sound behavior. This line of thinking is in bad taste at best, and potentially dangerous or life threatening at worst. It also has the potential to send a bad message to our youth, and it is making abhorrent behavior appear normal.

Words are like arrows that can cut you down. Words can also be uplifting. In that split second between saying what you want to say, in anger, pause to think better about it. Try, just for today, to take a second and be careful of what you say to someone else, even if that person is someone you might never see again or someone you love. When you speak with respect to someone, you will feel better about your choice, and you will feel better about yourself. You can go on to be the person who acts appropriately and is in control. Being discriminate with what you say, what you do, and how you feel is taking the high road, the road to authenticity and joy.

April 12

Affirmation: Today I will smile even though I don't feel much like it.

It appears to me that people aren't smiling as much. Perhaps it's when and where I have made this observation, but it seems that relatively young, attractive men and women aren't revealing their beautiful smiles. They walk around with frowns on their faces. I was so taken by this that I started saying, "Smile," to an attendant at the desk in the airport or the server at the local deli. Needless to say, they looked at me in bewilderment. Thankfully no one has punched me in the nose. Once in a while someone will hear me and recognize that they do need to smile more. Smiling through adversity and remaining positive when feeling down can only help a bad situation. What's really going on when you smile at someone? You are sending them joy, friendship, and love.

Practice frequent acts of smiling. Give someone a smile today. It may be all they receive that's good and kind. Did you know that it's easier to smile than not to and that smiling has been found to release powerful neurotransmitters like endorphins and serotonin, our body's natural feel-good drug? It's also been proven to improve your looks. Smiling is infectious. Not enough people smile. When I think about whether or not I'm smiling, I immediately make a concerted effort to smile in that very moment. Ready, set, smile. People will wonder what you're up to.

April 13

Affirmation: I am balanced and connected.

If it just so happens that you started reading affirmations today, or you are a seasoned pro, today contemplate, be reflective, perhaps you can focus on your ability to stay connected—connected to your peers, your family, your friends, your neighbors, and your faith. Perhaps you can work toward maintaining or developing greater balance in your life. Try not to focus on one particular aspect of your life, while giving little or no attention to other, very important, areas. Be healthy, eat fresh fruits and vegetables, stick to a consistent exercise plan that works for you, and get the right amount of rest to restore your overall well-being. Pray and meditate daily. These are the tools everyone speaks of. This is a formula that can work for you.

April 14

Affirmation: I have struggled and have learned what it takes to know joy.

Hope springs eternal only if that is what you have experienced or have been taught in word or deed. Patience is difficult for those who want what they want and want it now. Repentance is virtually unheard of for anyone who does not believe in taking responsibility for his or her own actions or who feels no remorse. Joy comes to those who struggle through and persevere. Growth provides a wondrous and virtuous feeling.

Patience is the key to joy. If everyone were born with the ability to be patient, the world would be a more peaceful place. Patience is something learned, especially if you are like me and find it hard to wait, be silent, and experience the peacefulness of the moment and not the urgency of your expression.

Decide what is important to you. What makes you happy? What makes the people around you happy? Are you contributing to or contaminating the situations in your life? What can you do to improve your relationships with friends, family, and yourself? You know what you need to stop or start doing. Think about it, and then, just for today, take what you have learned and put it to good use.

April 15

Affirmation: I feel great when I am complimented. Today I will compliment my loved ones and tomorrow a stranger!

Let's all try to praise more and be more encouraging to others. To be truly loved and appreciated means giving and receiving outward signs and positive affirmations. Compliments and praise are necessary, but don't forget the need to be shown that we are loved.

Love is a verb. It is not enough to tell someone how you feel; it is as important to show others by loving and caring acts of kindness. A compliment, taking a moment to recognize someone else's greatness, is an act of kindness that is beneficial to you, as well as others. Telling someone, "You rock!" may be just what that person needs to propel him or her into greatness.

April 16

Affirmation: Today I will do my best.

Mistakes from your past have the potential to cloud the moment. Worrying about the future can only lead to fear and apprehension. Try, at this very moment, to do your best. Whether that means doing something earth shattering or doing nothing at all, do the best you can at any given point in time. The next moment will come, and you will either go forward in your actions and thoughts or regress, but hopefully it will be your best.

All circumstances lead to change in our current state of awareness. Positive experiences can propel us to become better versions of ourselves. Negative awareness has the potential to bring us down and stop us in our tracks. The reality is that the present moment is all we have.

The plan, for you personally, is to rise to the level that makes you better. If you are doing well and moving in a positive direction, it doesn't mean you'll always feel this way. Life gets in the way, moods change, circumstances change, and people change. In this moment, set a higher standard, and raise the bar for yourself. Cultivate a path that moves you in the direction of your goals. You can always change and reevaluate your course at any time. In fact, it is good to change things up from time to time. This is your journey. This is my journey. This is our collective journey in life.

April 17

Affirmation: Today I will do what is necessary and then do a little more.

When I am busy with a project or planning an event, I feel compelled to let everything else go and focus on the task at hand. When I say I let things go, I am referring to what I least enjoy doing. You can always tell how I am doing, on any given day, by whether or not I made my bed. The key to living a peaceful existence, male or female, is to make your bed most days. If you share your space, do chores in cooperation with others. Your home can be an inviting, calming place that is not chaotic or in need of your immediate attention. The simplicity of taking care of the little things in life makes way for the possibility of doing great things. Do not put off what you know is a simple fix. If it means putting the cup in the sink, or filing up your gas tank when you know it is getting low, do it more often than not. Set routines and make balanced structure a habit. Give it a try. If I can do it, you can do it!

April 18

Affirmation: I stay connected with family and friends.

Estrangement is not an option. Are you guilty of giving up on a loved one, never speaking to that person again, and cutting him or her out of your life? How is that working for you? Anger, bitterness, resentment, hostility, fear, and abandonment—all these negative emotions arise from estrangement. Of course, we must walk away from relationships that are harmful and toxic. Herein lies the tough decision. When do we love someone through his or her difficulties, and when do we say, “Enough”? The answer is when leaving is the only option remaining. When you have done everything to make the relationship work and you are lovingly walking away or letting the person go from your life, it is with the best possible intentions. You can want the other person to change, but you can't make that person change. You might have to let go and move on to being your best self for you and your loved ones.

Trust and rely on others to help you through tough times with a spouse, a parent, or a child. We all are flawed, and we all need the grace and healing powers of love. Reach out, and give as much love to others as you can. A change for the better will happen.

April 19

Affirmation: Faith has the power to heal all worries.

Whenever I ask someone if they have faith, nine times out of ten they are taken totally off guard. "Faith? You mean do I go to church?" No, I mean do you have faith in something or someone other than yourself that can be a guide to knowing all is well and everything is as it should be? Faith knows that all is well within your heart, soul, and mind. For this to happen you must first let go of control and worry. Worrying is a waste of time and energy. It robs you of being the best you can be. Focus on what is happening in your life now. Worry over what is to come is senseless, because what you worry about hardly ever happens. When there is absolutely no proof that things will turn out for your benefit but you feel it in your heart and soul, that's faith.

April 20

Affirmation: Today I will give a smile away, and then another.

Practice frequent acts of smiling. Give someone a smile today. It may be all they receive that's good and kind. Did you know that it's easier to smile than not to and that smiling has been found to release powerful neurotransmitters like endorphins and serotonin, our body's natural "feel good" drug? It's also been proven to improve your looks. Smiling is infectious. Not enough people smile. When I think about whether or not I'm smiling, I immediately make a concerted effort to smile in that very moment. Ready, set, smile. That wasn't so hard now, was it?

April 21

Affirmation: Today I will get down to basics.

Let's all make a pact that today we will think and act in the most basic ways. "Basic" means no fluff, frills, pretenses, or extravagances. Getting down to basics is playing ball with a child instead of taking him on an elaborate play date that requires reservations at an upscale play place. Getting down to basics means turning off your cell phone and having a cup of coffee with a friend. Living simply is smelling the flowers, taking a walk in the rain, or having a hot fudge sundae, just because. Basic is holding a puppy or kitten. The most precious basics in life are a kiss, a hug, or holding hands. Telling someone you love him or her is the simplest way to live a beautiful life. Choosing the simplest way is the best way to become more peaceful and stress-free.

April 22

Affirmation: Today I will prepare for what I want to do next.

Indecision, not knowing whether to stay or go, can produce the most painful feeling of all. It is painful at times to live "in the meantime." Living in the meantime is a pause in our lives where we are not going forward or slipping behind. I believe this can be a time for personal growth, expansion and creativity. Pain and suffering are in the not knowing. Be at peace with the questions, and trust that the answers are already within you. You always know. Personal growth takes courage and vision. Most paths taken in life can be reversed and can be redirected. Not being proactive and changing the things you have control over, will only keep you stuck. Ease your burden by lifting someone else up. If everything is working for you at this moment, then there is no dilemma. Keep this thought handy for when you do need it. When you must go forward, make the choice you know is best and walk in the light.

April 23

Affirmation: Today I will look for what is possible.

Visions manifest through clear perception, adaptation, and balance. The word *vision* is associated with spirituality. *Vision* is defined as "being in a dream or trance." When I think of a vision, I think of what is to be, the future, something I conjure up that will manifest when the time is right, because that is what I will to happen. Of course, there will be variations, and things will come up that alter my vision to a larger or lesser degree. That goes without saying, but true visionaries set their sights on the future and make it happen. Think back to when you were young and saw yourself in a certain job or saw yourself having a spouse and children someday. Did those things happen for you? If not, did you change your vision to something that fit your situation better at that particular time in your life? The person who's become complacent and resolved just might end up in a place that no longer fulfills their needs, hopes, or desires. If this is resonating with you and you want to envision a different life for yourself, go for it. Think about what you are most passionate about, and do what it takes to realize that dream.

April 24

Affirmation: Today my goal is not to win, but to play fair.

Are you competitive? Do you want things to be perfect? Do you want to be in control of friends, family and just about everything around you? If this does not describe you, that's a good thing. (Perhaps it describes someone you know or love.) Perhaps you have this need or desire because you are scared, or feel that if you are not in control at all times, everything will fall apart. Remember—this does not necessarily have to be the case.

You have a right to have things the way you want and to be the master of your own ship, but you do not have the right to impose your beliefs or demands on others. Especially when it comes to relationships. We can't have things our way all the time. You can be right or you can be happy.

When compromise it difficult, take a step back and listen, really listen, to others and what *their* needs and wants are. Compromise is the key. That might mean "taking the high road" and letting someone else have a turn at wheel. Keep the lines of communication open and re-visit designated roles, as needed. Delegating, appropriating, coordination and cooperating fairly is the end goal, whether it is at work, with friends or loved ones.

April 25

Affirmation: Today I will give love unconditionally to those who love me and to those who don't.

To truly love, regardless of what life throws at you, is the greatest test of strength and fortitude. To love when you feel like you can't or shouldn't is tough. To love someone when that person is not doing what you think is best is hard. To love when you're furious is certainly trying at best. To love, no matter what, is an unbelievably difficult, arduous, and sometimes painful task. Yet it works! The proof is in the results. If you continue to love your family, your friends, and yourself and do not give up on them, everyone wins. Everyone gains. We all need our loved ones to love us through the hard times. We all need to be loved when we're not being our best selves. We need to be loved in spite of our insecurities and ridiculousness. When true joy and happiness meet love and tenderness, the sun shines and you are free to be a better and improved version of yourself.

April 26

Affirmation: The secret to getting things done is working together.

Even if you are engaged in a project that requires your undivided attention, and you think you are the only one that can get the job done, assistance from others is often warranted. When you are engaged in an activity, it always helps to get a second, or even a third opinion. There is strength in numbers.

When you're feeling overwhelmed and that you're in over your head, by all means speak up. Ask a trusted friend or co-worker. Go to your loved ones, especially your kids. Their perspective can be the most enlightening and thought provoking.

The saying goes, *united we stand, divided we fall.* The result of healthy, well-planned cooperation is peace, harmony and productivity. One purpose, one desire. Remember that when you ask for help and receive it lovingly, you are called to help others when the time comes. It's the way of the world.

April 27

Affirmation: I am willing and able to weather the storm.

The world has a strange way of presenting situations that will knock you down. When you get up—if you get up—a transformation occurs that actually makes a difference in your life and in the lives of those around you. If for some reason—perhaps fear or unwillingness—you are unable or choose not to see the signs to fix what is broken, the universe will wait until you're ready. Then, when the time presents itself, you will get a series of tests, another chance to get it right. Life is funny that way. The world cares about you and has your best interest at heart. If, however, you don't get it the first time, the universe will show up in different ways, sometimes in harsher, more demanding ways, to knock some sense in you again and again until you have the aha moment we've all been hearing about. Look out ... the universe is taking care of you!

April 28

Affirmation: Today I will notice the beauty in life.

When we're bored, we're not paying attention. Think about it ... when you pay attention, the experience can expand through your senses and beyond. When you pay attention to the ant building his home in the sand or to common objects and everyday occurrences, you are becoming aware. When you are receptive, you open yourself up to the full experience of seeing, smelling, hearing, tasting, and touching. The world begins to open up right in front of you. Smell the flowers, see the trees, feel the warmth of the sun, taste the sweetness of a peach, and hear the sound of the waves as you contemplate. Contemplate your dreams. Take notice, and be amazed.

April 29

Affirmation: Today I will take a walk.

Take a walk on a spring day. Take a walk on an autumn afternoon. Walk barefoot on the beach in the summer. And when winter comes, put on your snowshoes, and have fun! Why? Because it's good for you. Some people won't run or jump or swim. Even folks who are differently abled can take a walk with or without assistance.

Put your child in the baby carrier, and go around the block or to a park. Make certain you are dressed properly, and go out even though every fiber of your being doesn't want to. Take your pet for a walk. That's why we have pets—to make us better people! Walk with a friend who might be ill or needs to be with someone. Walk to the store or your city center to save on gas. It's better for the environment. Make walking a daily event. "You'll never walk alone."

April 30

Affirmation: I am open to happiness.
Today I will let it find me.

We all want to be happy. That's a given. We want to be happy because it feels amazing and it lets us know that all is right with the world. That all is right with our little corner of the world. Happiness, they say, is elusive. How then, do we obtain true happiness? Are we happy when someone or something makes us happy or is it a feeling we get inside when we are in a place of contentment? Perhaps we don't even know where or when happiness will find us. Perhaps it is like the elusive butterfly. Stop chasing it and it will come to you.

Today, be aware of when you are feeling safe and secure. Notice the smile on your face. Get in touch with the warm emotions you feel when you think about your loved one or a true friend. Realize that it just might take something simple like a song on the radio or a walk in the park to put you in a better mood, a happier mood. Just for today.

May

National Mental Health Month

May 1

Affirmation: I will take a moment to see and feel the beauty that surrounds me.

Close your eyes, and try to picture your surroundings. If you're at home, you can visualize the kitchen sink and the refrigerator or possibly your favorite chair. If you're at work, you might visualize your desk, the computer, or perhaps the door. What surrounds you can end up defining you if you are not careful.

If our surroundings are cheerful, organized, and comfortable, we come home to a place that invites serenity. If our space is plush and extravagant, it might make us feel successful and accomplished. If where we live or work is small but cozy and has everything we need, chances are we feel content and happy.

On the other hand, if you have let your surroundings go, there could be an overwhelming sense that there is something you have to do, something you must get done, hanging over your head. Our surroundings, whether we are aware of it or not, can make us uneasy or even angry. When the house is not tidy or "as it should be," there is a tendency to blame others and constantly nag them to clean their room or the garage, or any number of other possibilities. If someone collects too much stuff or has a problem throwing things away, then this problem can trickle down to other areas of his or her life.

Keeping your desk, your car, the yard, and your home as pleasant as possible can be as important as keeping your personal health and wellness intact. Where we live is where we love. Peace of mind and serenity lead to a greater ability to be happy with ourselves and not be so critical of others. Cooperation is important, as is a willingness and desire to make positive changes.

May 2

Affirmation: Today I will give up hating, and I will try again tomorrow.

Hate equals meanness—failing to do right and choosing to do wrong. Sin leads to shame, hurt, guilt, broken relationships, and so on. The opposite of hate is grace, forgiveness, kindness, caring, understanding, compassion, and so on. The Golden Rule dates back to the early teachings of Confucianism. "Do unto others, as you would have them do unto you." I think everyone would agree with that. But do we actually practice it in our daily lives?

Hate is a very bad concept. Nothing good comes from it. You might think hating someone is justifiable. It's not. You might think that if someone has egregiously harmed you, you have every right to hate him or her. Well, you're wrong. If you think you are justified in hating someone based on what he or she said or did, again you are wrong.

The good news, however, is that you can stop hating. You can let go of the hatred that's festering in your heart, your thoughts, and your spirit. You must stop hating. Stop hating for your family. Stop hating for your children. Stop hating for your friends and the community in which you live. Stop hating for future generations. Stop hating for you. Stop hating you.

May 3

Affirmation: I'm not afraid now. I'll wait until the time comes.

Talking about the time to be afraid makes me think of going to battle. What come to mind are health concerns. What comes to mind is having to change jobs. What comes to mind is anything that you have to do that scares you to death. Some things scare you that might not scare someone else. However, the reality is that there are milestones in your life that are frightening because of the unknown nature and the dramatic changes that will come as a result, whether good or bad. We all stress out over what's going to happen. Sometimes the fear is so great that we retreat. What Seneca said in the times of Nero and Ancient Rome is that what you are afraid of lessens when you are faced with the challenge. Put off your fear until the time is right. You might find you weren't that scared at all.

May 4

Affirmation: I am brave, I am strong, and I am smart.

You are braver than you give yourself credit for. You are super strong, and you are amazingly smart. How does that sound? There is absolutely no reason to think any less of yourself. You're the one and only person who truly knows your thoughts, your talents, and your potential. If you're not ready to proclaim your greatness, what's holding you back? Let go of the nonsense that is limiting you. You have much more going for you than you give yourself credit for. Just for today, think as if you have it all. You do have what it takes.

May 5

Affirmation: I know that the sky, the sea, and the earth need my admiration and my protection.

Apparently taking care of Mother Nature goes in cycles. Sometimes it is trendy, and other times it is just too much work and much easier to be thoughtless and careless. What happens to your spirit when you pick up a soda can or recycle your garbage? Do you get a warm feeling that you're doing something to protect the environment now and for future generations? What else can you do on a larger scale? Perhaps you could trade in your SUV for a more efficient compact car or look into solar panels and support the use of wind and solar energy. You know your conscience. Do what you can do, and then do a little more. God is watching.

May 6

Affirmation: Today I will look for the divine in people, places, and things, not forgetting the divine within me.

Open your eyes to the beauty in the world. Seeing a tree blossoming brings feelings of joy. A waterfall exudes power and force coupled with beauty. A wild cat in nature is pure and fierce at the same time. Did you know that God is there when you witness something that is truly awe-inspiring? God makes awe. God is the essence of nature and the overwhelming feelings of amazement and grandeur associated with it. The earth is as it should be. The ocean, the mountains, and the deserts are too vast to comprehend. They are God. They are splendor. Take good care.

May 7

Affirmation: If I want to change another person, I must first change myself.

Lead by example. Relationships are so fragile. A large contributor to unhappiness is when one person tries to change the other. We all change and hopefully grow into wiser, more contented people. That's the goal. But for many, stress and unhappiness leads to addiction, infidelity, physical ailments, or failure.

What can you do for that person you love? Be a role model. Strive every day to work on yourself. Make trying to improve yourself your goal. If the other person is given room and time to improve and does transform, be thankful. If the other person is unable to change thoughtfully and carefully, make your decision either to be with that person or to not be with that person. Throughout the process keep clear and consistent boundaries, and take care of yourself. Be fair, be kind, and be inspiring.

May 8

Affirmation: I choose to make peace with my past decisions.

Why regret what you said or did in the past? If your intentions were mean-spirited, you can apologize and ask for forgiveness, but you can never take back your actions or words. You can repent and make amends. Doing so will bring you peace. When you look back over your life, you will see the missed opportunities as growing experiences. Think of the hard times as hurdles you overcame. Look at those negatives, and chalk them up to life experience. Don't let your failures define you. Perhaps your bad times weren't that bad after all.

May 9

Affirmation: I will stop being so hard on myself.

In our darkest hour, we are our own judge and jury. We suffer and put ourselves down. We think the worst and can't understand why others don't see things our way. Inevitably, someone will come up to you and tell you that things aren't so bad. *It isn't as bad as you think.* That's because to someone else, it isn't as bad as *they* think! Personal failures and mistakes are hard to live with. Loss, grief, sorrow, and pain can be overwhelming and all-consuming at times. People recognize that.

What others know, which you might not, is that once you stop being so hard on yourself and begin to look at the situation in a different light, you can then begin to stop torturing yourself. Let go of the pain. Move forward. Life is full of lessons. When it is seemingly impossible to get out of a bad situation, ask for help and seek out consolation from family, friends, or professional counselors. Our pain should never be in vain.

May 10

Affirmation: I will choose a day this week to have nothing to do and take all day to do it!

There are seven days in a week, and one is set aside for rest. Everyone needs their batteries recharged, and rest is needed as much as eating right and exercising. Can you do nothing except breathe? Can you sit quietly and rid your mind of the noise and chaos around you? If you are the type of person who's constantly on the go, this form of meditation might be a foreign concept to you. Not only will you not be able to slow down and stop, but also chances are that you won't even know why you would want to. Rest and alone time are the prescriptions for stress, worry, and anxiety. A calm mind is able to make better decisions and to think in a more clear and relaxed manner. Being frantic and always doing something—anything—are counterproductive. Today try to relax whenever possible, take a breath, and let go of any tension or stress.

May 11

Affirmation: Today when I fall, I will get up and keep going.

Do you do everything by the book? Do you do everything you're supposed to do? Let it go for once. Let go of the need to follow the rules. Of course, there are times when the rules must be obeyed, but there is also room for free thinking and going beyond what you normally do. A toddler knows how to walk without an instruction manual. Trust yourself and your intuition. Trust your instincts and your better judgment. Trust your own decision-making abilities, and when the opportunity presents itself, go it alone. Give it a shot.

May 12

Affirmation: I strive to do the best I can at what I love.

Striving to accomplish something so cool in life that people can't take their eyes off you is very poetic. It almost sounds decadent. It's as if you want the spotlight to be on you. Well, come on—maybe you do a little bit. When you perform in front of a crowd, you have the satisfaction of knowing you entertained people. You can tell by the applause. But what about when you make an amazing apple pie or help a child with their homework? It's nice to be appreciated and congratulated on how awesome you are. We are keenly aware of other people who do things that we'll never be able to do. Or if you can do what they do, you will never be able to do it quite the same way. When you see someone who loves what he's doing, give that person a "Way to go!" Let him know that, in that moment, you couldn't take your eyes of him.

May 13

Affirmation: Today I'll create a blessed day.

I remember the first time I had a discussion with a friend about humility. It was a moment definitely worth remembering. I had to take the time to find out what being humble meant to me. I had never thought about it before, and I thought I knew pretty much all there was to know about myself. Pretty arrogant, huh? So I looked it up. *Humility* is defined as "having a clear perspective and, therefore, respect for one's place in context." Being humble is being well grounded. Humility is intrinsic self-worth when it comes to relationships and your perspective on whom and where you are in life. What a humbling lesson to learn. I am truly humbled by my friends and family and for the people in my life who make me better.

May 14

Affirmation: Today I will try to not do or say anything that does not bring joy.

The sun shines universally. The sun coming up in the morning and setting in the evening are colossal reminders that life goes on. You are provided for. Everything is available to you if you're receptive. Flowers and trees aren't fussy. They don't refuse light when it's provided. They accept what's required to grow and be amazing. Why then is it so difficult, for so many, to ask for assistance or to receive help?

If you're not currently in need, are you the provider who steps out of your daily routine and gives to others? It's an amazing feeling to be the receiver and the recipient of love, kindness, and understanding. Providing for others in their time of need is essential. Those who have received help are keenly aware of how life altering it is and how thankful they are. Once you are back on your feet, turn it around and pay it forward.

May 15

Affirmation: Letting go does not mean giving up.

Anger, hurt, and resentment are emotions generally directed to the people to whom we are closest. When we feel hurt or slighted, the natural tendency seems to be to get angry and lash out.

Perhaps you are guilty of misdirected or misguided negativity. Perhaps you take your anger out on someone who has nothing to do with your pain and is innocent and underserving of your wrath. Or maybe you're the type of person who says nothing and bottles it all up inside until you explode or experience depression and anxiety. The pent-up emotions that you have not dealt with will manifest physical and emotionally and will shut you down. Talk to someone, and get help if needed. Insight and self-awareness will show up.

May 16

Affirmation: "Hi, present moment, nice to be with you!"

I often wonder why my day typically unfolds so differently from what I thought it would be like when I woke up that morning. Whenever someone asks me how I'm doing, I generally reply, "I'm fine, thank you. Check back with me again later." Hopefully your daily plans go the way you want them to. Even if your situation is not ideal, try starting the day by thinking today will be great.

We all want our days to be good ones, but as we all know, from time to time life can throw us curveballs. When you plan a day at the beach and your child comes down with a fever, when you are at work and nothing is going right, or when you have more work dumped on your desk just as you are about to leave the office, your mood can abruptly change. There are literally thousands of possibilities that can turn your day sour. As many ways as it can go wrong, there are as many possible ways to make it better and keep you on track.

What's most important is what you learn from your disappointment and how flexible you are at turning a bad situation around. We often get stuck in the misery because we feel hurt, let down, or taken advantage of. *It's not fair. Why me?* "Why me?" is a place in which a lot of people hang out. It's called playing the victim. Whatever happened to ruin your day is over, and what remains is the choice to not let it affect you, move on, and be better for it.

Learn from what is going on, and enjoy the present moment. Forget about what isn't, and focus on what is. This is your moment.

When you keep an objective perspective, you can be more productive and more receptive to joy. Enjoy the moment in the moment, and walk away a winner. In the evening, when you reflect on the happenings of your day, put it all into perspective, laugh about it, and then let it go. Trust me. You'll have plenty to think about again tomorrow.

May 17

Affirmation: I will strive to be compassionate and keep my temper in check.

When you are angry with someone, it is his or her behavior, not the person, that you have a problem with. You are angry because what is going on resonates with you. What makes one person angry may not anger another person. Therefore, the best course of action is to become fully aware of what upsets you. It is your job to recognize what can set you off, what your triggers are. Is it when someone interrupts you or you find yourself standing in line for too long? Work on the issues, and then when someone offends, you will be less reactive, less explosive. You will be more likely to act in a non-offensive way, keeping your anger in check. Anger is one of the most difficult emotions to control. Anger issues require management. Perhaps you don't have the tools to deal with your anger, because you were not taught how to deal with your emotions as a child. Girls are taught not to get angry, and boys are taught to let it out on the playing field. Perhaps you were shown how to act out in anger. We are taught any number of ways to deal with our anger, talking it out generally not being one of them.

If we can teach our girls and boys by words and by example how to handle what to say and how to react when they are mad, then we are all invested in working toward a better future. On the other hand, if we model how to scream and fight, aggression and stupidity will flourish.

May 18

Affirmation: Today I will let go of the "old" me.

We pigeonhole ourselves and limit our potential. Why? Fear mostly. Consciously we limit ourselves, because if we don't put ourselves out on a limb, we risk nothing. To the contrary, we all know that risk, taking a gamble on ourselves, has the potential to go very badly. That's true.

However, if you can let go of the limiting expectations you have for yourself, you will be able to recognize that, although the limitations you put on yourself are preconceived, they have an origin in that past that you still cling to. Parents, siblings, teachers, and friends can define you if you let them. The words they use to describe you stay with you until you give up and give in. If you let go of the criticism (such as being told you were not good enough to be what it was you wanted to be), then you will have the room to take off and soar. It's only when you turn off that little voice inside your head that holds you back that you can flourish and be happy. Yes, be happy. Be happy.

May 19

Affirmation: I am present. I show up for life.

Shift happens. Have you left yourself behind? Are you not fully engaged in your life? What is missing in your life could possibly be your enthusiasm, courage, or passion. Inertia possibly has set in. Perhaps you've given up on the hope that you can be what you want to be and that you can live a purposeful and meaningful life. What is missing in your life? Is it your dream job? Do you long for a loving, healthy relationship? Perhaps it is as basic as health and wellness for you and your family. At this moment your life is what it is. However, changes are inevitable. Perhaps you can get what you want when you need it, not necessarily when you want it. Because you haven't gotten what you want up to now, you shut down and get discouraged.

The fact is you must regain faith in yourself and the world around you. Trust in yourself, and start making better decisions when it comes to what you need to fill the void in your life. While you are on your journey you might find that something different pops up for you—a different opportunity than you had anticipated or something better that you hadn't thought of. If it feels right, do it. Don't miss out on the life you were destined to live. You can always seek help and guidance along the way.

May 20

Affirmation: Today I will stay focused.

Just when you're on the path to feeling better and getting things accomplished for a change, something always shows up to give you pause. Are you the type of person who, when the smallest interruption comes along, stops what you're doing and starts something else? Not all the time, but usually it happens when you're engaged in something that you're not crazy about doing in the first place. For some, distraction can come in many forms, and it can happen enough times to shut you down and count you out if you let it.

Learn to keep focused on the goal at hand. The key (and it is vital to being successful) is that if you find yourself giving up, try again. Get back on track each and every time. When you walk away from something, do it because it's in your best interest to change course, not because you've lost heart. Does this sound familiar? Months go by, and you still have something going on that you have left undone. Unresolved issues result in incomplete feelings that can be daunting.

Perhaps things need to be more orderly and manageable for you. Perhaps you need the allotted time and tools to finish the project. Perhaps you need to know that no matter the outcome, you did a great job. If obstacles come, you can jump over them. Go around them, or move them out of the way. Whatever you do, don't let them slow you down.

May 21

Affirmation: The next time I am angry at someone I will look at what I have done first.

When we are angry with someone, it's not the person who causes our anger; it's what that person said or did that triggers feelings of anger in us. Something a person says or does can trigger negative thoughts, feelings, and reactions in us.

Anger is a normal emotion, but not a favorable one. Before you blame other people or accuse them of causing your foul mood, take time to examine their intentions and what is really going on. What is it that is striking a chord with you? At the same time, take a look at what is happening with you and why you are reacting so strongly.

Are you overly stressed or in a less-than-optimal place in your life? Are you tired and, therefore, easily irritated? It may be that both sides are guilty of being wrong in the moment and perhaps not being in control of their behavior. Nothing is ever one-sided. If we look at what angers us in a different way, a way in which we take responsibility for our actions or reactions, then we might see that a bad situation can be turned around. Get the facts. Take responsibility. Let go of negativity. If it's not possible to come to a conclusion, walk away knowing you did your best.

May 22

Affirmation: I declare I can accomplish anything I set my mind and heart to do.

Why do you get stuck? Why do you think you are inartistic, incompetent, non-analytical, uncoordinated, or not funny? You name it. Fill in the blanks. What is it that you tell yourself? I am not ________________________________.

I am ________________________________.

Could it be possible that what you tell yourself is exactly what you desire to be? You can't dance. You can dance if you choose to dance. You choose not to dance. You choose not to learn to dance. You feel embarrassed when you dance and, therefore, refuse to try. Dancing makes you feel uncomfortable. Exchange the word *dance* for whatever it is you tell yourself you can't do. Here's the key. You can do most things you say you can't. You can sing, and you can be analytical, but for some reason you choose not to be. Maybe you think you aren't physically or mentally able to do what others can do. This is possibly the exception to the rule. You judge yourself critically without even trying. Lighten up. No one cares if you do things well or if you are a beginner. You have to do bad art before you can do good art. Practice what you think you aren't that good at, and when you improve, give yourself a high five and a pat on the back. Accomplishment is a true joy in life.

May 23

Affirmation: I strive to be good. It's a God-and-me thing.

Be good, and do well. Studies show that when given the choice, it is instinctual to go down the wrong path and has been since early civilization. Why? It's far more thrilling and, therefore, more enjoyable to be naughty.

Another possible factor in making wrong choices is our well-intentioned friends. Misery loves company. "If I'm going to break the rules, come along and join me." This is when conflict arises. Do I do what I want regardless of the repercussions, or do I walk away and do the right thing?

The answer to that question is as old as time and is uniquely individual.

Breaking the rules is not just for the young. Broken relationships and failed career paths are examples of bad decision-making. Taking the high road perhaps is not appealing; taking the low road is a lot more fun.

Saints, poets, and prophets exemplify how to live a loving, well-intentioned, and virtuous life. Mother Teresa of Calcutta is an example of a selfless and blessed life. She lived and worked among the sickest and poorest people of the world. I look to her for wisdom and strength. The way to live, in my book, is simple: strive to be good and do better each day with the help of grace.

May 24

Affirmation: I allow myself to be led by my soul.

The soul is your essence. It is who you are. When you release your desires, your spirit takes flight, you are without inhibition, and you truly have fun. The soul is the source of creativity, beauty, passion, and love. You know when you are in a soulful moment. The problem is that most of us are not in touch with our souls as much as we could be or as much as we should be. Society doesn't promote the importance of soul work. If you survey a group of folks, most people won't even be able to tell you what the soul is. Soul food, soul sounds, food for the soul—all may be hard to describe but easy to recognize.

What are you feeling when you are in a soulful place? Feelings are what make you unique. Some philosophers say the soul is where the divine resides. Perhaps you've let go of the concept of having a soul. If this is true for you, please consider reexamining your soulful self. Peace and joy will find you and will reside in you forever.

May 25

Affirmation: Today I will put (name) ____________________ at the top of my "most wanted" list!

When we feel wanted, appreciated, and accepted, we thrive and flourish. We bloom and blossom in an atmosphere of warmth and caring. When nurturance is missing, however, the temperature drops from cold to freezing. Oftentimes, in relationships, people fail to follow a basic psychological and spiritual principle that gives the other person what they want most—a sense of fulfillment, a sense of wanting to be wanted, and a sense of being appreciated. If these basic needs are not met, there is a tendency to grow apart and become isolated and alienated. Sometimes we wait for the other person to make the first move. "If you loved me you would appreciate me more without me having to tell you!" Healthy communication is the key to any successful relationship. Communicating your needs and wants in a loving and kind way fosters understanding and clarity.

When a child grows up feeling unappreciated or unwanted, he or she is not learning the basic principles of how to love and be loved. Self-love and loving and respecting yourself and others must be taught and reinforced. Caregivers must examine their own personal set of circumstances and biases. If they have not felt wanted, loved, or appreciated themselves, the road ahead is much more difficult.

The good news is the cycle can be broken. Perhaps you are kind and loving toward others, but you know someone who isn't. You can teach by example and help that person. Put him or her on the top of your "most wanted" list. If you are a giver and a helper, you have the power and the potential to introduce a new start and a fresh beginning to someone who needs healing. If you need healing, seek out those who can help you and lift you up. It goes both ways.

May 26

Affirmation: Today I will open my mind and soften my heart.

One of the greatest obstacles that stands in the way of achieving great things is thinking that what you want to do is "impossible." What that translates into is "I can't." "I can't" translates into "I don't want to," which turns into "I won't" or "I'm afraid to." When we focus on the negative, chances are we can't and we won't. We find ourselves closed off to new possibilities. Our hearts and minds are walled off. We see a task or a situation that we think is too much for us, over our head, or out of reach, when we perhaps need to change our way of thinking and tell ourselves, "Maybe I can handle this." Give it a try. Challenges broken down into smaller step are more doable and generally more successful.

Sometimes we discover joy, not by seeking it out directly but as a by-product of something else. Achievement and accomplishment take consistent movement. When a task or situation seems daunting or impossible, keep an open mind and do not harden your heart. The impossible can turn into that which is possible!

May 27

Affirmation: Today, I will be respectful to others. I will benefit in return.

We gain respect when we simply are ourselves and are not trying to be someone we're not. When we act genuinely, people are more likely to act in a positive and therefore, respectful manner. No one respects a phony! The opposite, naturally, is disrespect. Disrespect is anger charged and comes from a place of annoyance and disappointment from the person you are interacting with respect is not something set-aside solely for individuals. We are taught to respect certain groups of people, such as our elders, our teachers and employers, people of authority in general. I suggest, as a culture, we would all benefit immensely by taking respect a step further to include people of different nations, different abilities, sexual orientation, creeds and colors. On the surface, if we lead with conduct that warrants regard for another human being we can then avert animosity, hatred and division in our interactions moving forward,

I leave you with the most important kind of respect – self-respect. Be good to yourself today and treat yourself with dignity. Others will follow.

May 28

Affirmation: Today, when I think I have done my best, I will do more.

When stressed, worried, depressed, or anxious, we often let things go. We might do as little as possible or find ourselves doing nothing at all. We find ourselves powerless, unmotivated, and unwilling. In troubled times, we are unable to do the things we need to be doing or want to be doing. It is in these moments that it's important to rise above the inertia and the feelings of inadequacy and incompetence and do our best.

"Always do your best." The irony is that when you feel down, you do less, and this is just what will get you out of a slump. The universe is always testing you. People who are highly motivated and get through the day with a sense of accomplishment are physically, spiritually, and mentally more balanced than those who put off until tomorrow, wish a magic fairy will come, or just don't care anymore and have given up hope.

Apathy leads to lethargy. It's when you least want to go for that run that you must. It's when you least want to tackle that project on your desk that calls to you that you should. It is that phone call home that will change the course of your day simply by ticking it off your to-do list. What is it that you need to do today that you have been putting off? One step at a time brings the level of negativity one step closer to balance.

May 29

Affirmation: Today I will have an attitude of gratitude.

Happy people are thankful. Thankful people are happy. If you practice gratitude, the results are joyous. Is it difficult for you to feel happy most times? How often do you feel unhappy? Do you often feel like the victim, as if something is being done to you or that your misery is someone else's fault and not your own? Life is hard. It's not always easy. Not easy at all. But the life you are given is a gift to you.

Each day you have a new opportunity to make the best of your situation and work with what you have, not with what you wish you had. You don't have what you want all the time. You have what you have. The thing about life is that you have a chance each and every day to take the circumstances of your life and make them better. Design them the way you want your life to be. Take that class, or go back to school. Reassess the people with whom you associate. And by all means, if you are involved in destructive patterns, this may be your moment to stop.

Be thankful for your ability to change, and then do it. Let go of old, destructive habits, and create new, healthier ones.

May 30

Affirmation: Today I will try to practice what I preach.

This will resonate within the heart and soul of the healer. Whether you are a doctor, nurse, dietitian, health instructor, clergy, or parent, the saying goes, "Practice what you preach." I instruct most, if not all, of my patients to eat well, exercise, take vitamins, drink plenty of water, meditate, and journal daily. How difficult is this to do every day?

The minute you get off course and eat sugar, for example, it's very difficult to get back on track. Often being on track is boring and no fun. What is the price of being healthy and well adjusted? For those who battle anxiety and depression, perhaps doing just what does not come easy is the answer. When feeling overwhelmed and unappreciated, do you tend to do everything that is counterproductive to feeling better? Do you indulge in oversleeping, overeating, sugar, alcohol, or smoking? If you want your loved one to be at a healthy weight, practice good eating habits and develop your personal wellness plan. If you want your kids to get better grades in school, let them see you reading a book. Lead by example. Change starts within the body, mind, and soul of you, the healer.

May 31

Affirmation: Today I will be happy with the chaos and upheaval in my life, knowing that pain and confusion are signs of discovery.

Perhaps the chaos in my life can be an impetus for positive change. It's an easy concept yet difficult to grasp if you are in the mist of upheaval in your life. Think about it for a moment. If everything in your world is running smoothly, chances are you won't have a desire to change or make things better. You are perfectly happy with the way things are. Chances are it is only in troubled times and when your life is spiraling out of control that you find yourself contemplating making changes to get out of your current situation and into something new and different—better. If everything in life stayed the same, there would be no growth, no improvement. When you leave a relationship because it is no longer working for you, look around and find someone new who meets your needs and makes you happier. It is the same thing with your job or career path. How often have you been unhappy in a position, when just around the corner you found a much better position? And so it goes. I offer to you that if you are willing to recognize the "the swirl of chaos" and see it as an impetus for change, your life will be enhanced by no longer fearing the times of trial and tribulations but welcoming the bad times, as well as the good. As always, surround yourself with people who lift your spirit and who support you in a positive way.

June

Children's Awareness Month

June 1

Affirmation: I know what is worth keeping in my life.

You can't do good art until you do bad art. I've said this before, and I'll say it again. It takes a beginner's mind to be proficient at anything in life. Creativity takes time, patience, and commitment. You must try different strategies, different ways of doing things, and look at your work from time to time with a critical eye. You have to examine and reexamine. When you have realized your vision, you know you have something to be proud of.

So it is in life. Knowing what to stay with and what to walk away from is never easy. You struggle with getting rid of the things that clutter your life. Think about what you can live without and what your life would be like without it. The negativity in your life is the first thing that has to go.

June 2

Affirmation: Let it be.

So many need to feel a sense of control in their lives. Control of their family, their workplace, and their environment is so important to their existence. Perhaps you or someone you know needs to be in control at all times. The need to control everything only sets you up for failure. The struggle to control, the pursuit of having things exactly the way you want them, is endless and fruitless.

You have no control over the people in your life. You do, however, have control of how you think and react. If things aren't going the way you want them to, change the way you view the situation. Change the way you think. If you change your reaction and change the way you normally feel, things will go much smoother and you will be much happier.

June 3

Affirmation: I do me better than anyone else.

I am the best me I can be. Nobody does you better than you! When you go somewhere unfamiliar, or you're with people you are meeting for the first time, it's tempting to act differently from the way you normally would. Perhaps you have an inclination that this time you will speak up more, or this time you will talk less.

Whatever it may be, there's always something that you'll find to improve. It's a constant search for that one thing that will make you look better or something that will make others like you more. This type of thinking, of course, is not healthy. The trick is to be *in like* with yourself; others will follow. Instead of trying to be someone you're not, try being you. You might get some lighthearted teasing or ribbing at times. It's how you handle the awkwardness that defines your personality.

We're all flawed. Being a first-rate version of you means allowing yourself to be vulnerable. Don't give the past permission to hold you back. You are who you are, and you are great. Love yourself, and be good to yourself. It feels really good.

June 4

Affirmation: I have what it takes!

Being able to relax is truly balanced living. When thinking about your life, it can be easy to sell yourself short. However, you're smarter than you think you are. You can take that class and go back to school. You can make important decisions without having to run them by anyone first

You are braver and stronger than you think. Perhaps you were warned as a child not to do certain things because they're dangerous and you might get hurt. Well, yes, you might get hurt, but that's no reason not to try something. On the other hand, you might not get hurt. This leads to a lot of what-if thinking. Being strong and brave simply means that you weigh the possibilities and proceed with caution. You have what it takes.

June 5

Affirmation: Today I will remain calm and be open to love.

There are triggers that signal uneasiness for everyone. My trigger is driving. I am bothered when people cut me off or tailgate. I am bothered when I see people driving carelessly and not paying attention. I get angry when drivers are inconsiderate.

What are the triggers that prevent you from remaining calm? Are you even aware of what makes you upset, or are you so far beyond caring that you've become complacent and resolved to the fact that your life is full of stress anyway so why bother?

Seekers of wisdom and men and women of faith live not only for their own enlightenment but to make others' days a little bit brighter. Listen to what they're saying. Observe how they strive to live each moment with mindful awareness and open hearts.

Slow down. Stop worrying. Be aware every day that nothing is going to happen that you are not prepared to handle with courage, love, and an open mind. Open your mind to the possibility of love.

June 6

Affirmation: I give hugs. I need hugs!

I used to say that with twelve hugs a day, you're mentally healthy. Now it's down to eight! I'm a hugger. I hug everybody. Are you a hugger? I suppose one is either a hugger or not. I don't discriminate against non-huggers, but I have to say I don't understand them. Why don't people like to be hugged? It's extremely awkward to give a hug to a non-hugger. Perhaps that's why non-huggers don't hug. They're afraid to take the risk and hug another non-hugger. I respect a non-hugger's right not to hug. However, I never know if a person is a hugger or not. Mostly they are, and I'm safe. I'm sending you a hug. Go out today, and give (or receive) seven more.

June 7

Affirmation: Today I will make the best of whatever situations come my way.

A good day is a day without drama. It's a pleasant day when things go relatively smoothly. You wake up feeling terrific, and the feeling lasts throughout the day. However, a perfect day perhaps comes along once in a blue moon. Times when the circumstances in your life are lined up, everyone is happy, you're happy, and everything is right with the world do happen from time to time, but not all the time.

Life has its ups and downs. Living comes with pain and suffering. What you do with your life and how you handle the hard times are what make you unique. What brings out the best in you is determined by your attitude toward life.

Your attitude is your personal view of life. It's how you feel about your circumstances. If you aren't happy about the way your life is headed, you can make changes and set a new course for yourself. If your life right now isn't perfect, you have the ability in the meantime to change the way you view your circumstances.

You have a life to live. You can do this. You can make the best of your situation. Why not? The alternative is being miserable and nasty and walking around with a bad attitude. Today, try to see the good in your surroundings. Create a good day.

June 8

Affirmation: When change comes into my life, I know I'm being tested. I'll be good to myself.

When you're being tested, you're faced with situations when your decision-making abilities, your courage, and your sensibilities are in question. When faced with change, it's important not to rush into anything. Take your time, get the facts, weigh the options, seek counsel, and then make the choice that is best for you. Only you will know if you are doing what is in your best interest.

When faced with a major decision in life, you must lead with your heart, your mind, and your soul. Decision-making can be extremely difficult, stressful, and anxiety producing. It can be overwhelming. You can become stuck.

Try to be as healthy as possible. Be physically balanced by eating healthy foods, exercising, and getting enough rest. Try to be emotionally and spiritually balanced through the practice of meditation and being with friends and family for support. Take your time; don't rush to judgment. Make decisions when you are feeling capable and competent. There are good times to make adjustments and very bad times to make them. Take your time. When the light is green, it's your turn to cross the street.

June 9

Affirmation: I am growing old to feel young again.

I enjoy my age. I don't look back and wish I were ten years younger. The reason is that there's nothing I can't do now that I could do then, taking into consideration that increased physical limitation is normal and natural. If I want to do something, age is not a factor. I am happier and in a better place than I was before. I live my life in the moment and not in the past. I wouldn't want to go back. I am enjoying my self in the here and now.

If you give up on life and happiness, you have lost the race. You have pain, suffering, and loss in your life. Just as you found your answers before, life is waiting for you to jump back in. Get enthusiastic about your life no matter how young or old you are.

June 10

Affirmation: Today I will look for the silver lining.

Finding something good in every day is a challenge. When something bad happens, it's overwhelming and it has the potential to erase everything good that has happened previously. We all have a tendency to complain and fixate on what's bad, because it usually comes out of nowhere and throws us off.

On any given day you are faced with difficult challenges. On those days there might be a moment when you take a walk or see a child holding his or her mom's hand, or perhaps someone tells you that you are doing a good job. Maybe you have a nice talk with a friend. Whatever it is, there are times throughout your day that are fun, happy, loving, or silly. Use the good times in your day to counter what didn't go well. Look for joy. Don't let the bad times win.

June 11

Affirmation: When I say something bad about someone or something, I will replace it with something good.

It's not always easy to say the right thing. It's not always easy to think the right thing. It certainly isn't always easy to do the right thing.

Life is hard, but it's not impossible. Life can be easier if you make a conscious decision to replace the negativity in your life with more positive thoughts and actions. When you catch yourself saying or thinking something that you know is hurtful or wrong, stop right there and cut it out. That's right—cut it out. Say something nice. Break the habit by breaking the mold. Sometimes the less said, the better. Try to live by that simple motto.

June 12

Affirmation: I will keep trying. I won't give up.

I am impatient. I know this about myself. Sometimes I just can't wait. When I am able to stick with something and give it my all, the results are always good. Backing out and giving up rarely feel right. If you are impatient, you'll never get to where you need to be if you don't persevere in life.

We've all heard a thousand times, "If at first you don't succeed, try, try again." As you get busy with your life, there is a tendency to look at things as too difficult, too expensive, or too much trouble. Ask yourself if you would have backed down that easily ten or fifteen years ago. If the answer to your question is no, then what is holding you back now? Start with baby steps if necessary.

Knowing when to let go is as important as knowing when to hold on tight. However, the key to getting ahead is to stick with your intention. Don't give up until you have the results you want. Don't stop until you're done. It's that easy. It's also easy to get distracted. If you keep up what you're doing, the end result will be that much sweeter. It's fun to run the race. It's great to win. The real joy is in crossing the finish line.

June 13

Affirmation: Today I will turn my dreams into goals and my goals into reality.

What do you dream of having? Who do you dream of becoming? Where do you dream of living? Who do you want to be with? Is it possible that you've lost sight of your dreams due to complacency?

Some may say, "My situation is fine, and I am in a place that's all right for now. Why dream of things I can't have?" This type of thinking might sound familiar to you. If not, then you're one of the lucky ones who've experienced the thrill, joy, amazement, and even miracle of having your dreams come true. Take one day at a time, one dream at a time.

No one keeps you from realizing your dreams but you. What is it that you want out of life? Write it on a slip of paper. Keep it close to you. Now that you know what you want, what's next? What do you need to do, whom do you need to help you, and what needs to change for you to get to where you want to be? These questions could be holding you back. The answers will propel you forward. Take action. You have to have the courage to step out of your comfort zone and change whatever it is in your life that's not working. It's up to you. You have that dream in your pocket. Take it out, and dust it off.

June 14

Affirmation: I am creative.

We are all creative, and we all have imaginations. You might not be aware that you have an eye for design, beauty, fashion, writing, gardening, or woodworking—all talents that require an artistic flair.

It's common to compare yourself to that kid in school who was so good at art, dance, or music that even being around him or her was so intimidating that you gave up on your best efforts.

You know what's beautiful and what's not. Draw on that vision from time to time. Don't ignore your creative side or make excuses for it. The artist in you can create watercolor paintings, music, song, dance, sculpture, or even metalworking. The list goes on. What is it that you can imagine yourself doing? If you can imagine your creation, you can imagine the artist in you. Like any other muscle in your body, creativity must be exercised.

June 15

Affirmation: The less said, the better.

Most people either talk too much or rarely talk at all. Some people talk just to hear themselves think. For some, talking too much can be a result of anxiety or low self-esteem—so much so that they can't stop even if they wanted to. This might seem extreme, but many people suffer from "talking-too-much-itis."

Knowledge is a plus in any conversation. Without knowledge of a situation, you talk and have no idea what you are talking about. This can be extremely awkward. Whenever you are unfamiliar with a topic, take a breath and listen to what others are saying. If you feel you have something to contribute to the conversation, by all means speak up. But if you're not fully engaged and are preoccupied with what you are planning to say next, chances are you will not be putting your best foot forward.

The art of conversation is just that, an art form. To improve our quality of life and relationships, we all need to know when to talk and when not to talk.

June 16

Affirmation: Today I will decide what is important to me and what it is I am here to do.

Mark Twain said, "The two most important days in your life are the day you are born and the day you find out why." Are you looking forward to the next chapter of your life, the next phase? When, you were young, your parents told you, "You're just going through a phase." They were right, and that's a good thing.

What phase of life are you in now? Are you seeking an education, a career path, family life, or possibly retirement? Do you now have the time and resources to pursue those goals? Are you ready? Ready or not, it's time to move on. Live your life out loud. Have fun. Think of yourself as a kid again, one just going through a phase. Life is good.

June 17

Affirmation: Today, when I come to the finish line, I will look for the next starting gate.

Everything has a beginning and an end. When you get to the end it's easy to think, *That's it. That's all there is.* Perhaps the end of one thing may be the beginning of something else. It could be something better. Get a fresh start. Life is a series of "get up and do it again." Endurance is perseverance. Never give up. Run your race, and then keep on going.

Never give up on the people you love, the relationships in your life, your family, or yourself. Take life in stride. Sometimes you are faster and stronger than other times. Sometimes you have to rest and take it easy. The key to lasting happiness is not to give up on life. Never stop loving, caring, or being good to yourself. You'll come out on top every time. You'll be the winner, no matter what.

June 18

Affirmation: I am responsible for me. There's no one else to blame.

After football, the most popular sport in this country is the blame game. People say, "It wasn't my fault. It was him or her." We blame others so we look good. We blame so as not to have to deal with the consequences. We blame for many reasons. High on that list is not having to take responsibility for your actions.

There really is no need for blame. The past is gone. The deed was done. Who cares who did it anyway? Clean up the mess, try not to do it again, and move on. (If it is a criminal act, of course you must be aware of who is guilty.) Not blaming yourself or others requires knowing that everyone is human and everyone makes mistakes. Teach by example, and let the children of tomorrow grow up to know the importance of taking responsibility for what they do wrong, as well as what they do right.

June 19

Affirmation: Today I will practice remembering only good things.

We all would like to improve our memory. There are a number of ways to do this, such as creating word associations, saying a name several times during and after meeting someone, or creating images in your mind that help you to remember. It can be very helpful to have a photographic memory that immediately recognizes and recalls relevant information quickly and easily. That, however, is extremely uncommon. Your memory can be sharp and quick or slow and forgetful at times.

A good memory retains information on people, places, and things. A healthy memory learns from past mistakes and triumphs. A kind memory recalls others fondly. What you hold onto in your mind creates either a positive or negative foundation for how you have gotten to this good point in your life, and it provides a road map for where you are headed.

A good memory comes in two forms: recognizing the positive, affirming, happy, whole, and healthy occurrences and events; and recognizing that even though you would not have intentionally chosen some of the things that have happened to you, the outcome helped to create who you are today in a way that would not otherwise have come about.

June 20

Affirmation: I am confident.

The key to being a winner is having confidence—in yourself and in the people with whom you surround yourself. Have confidence that no matter the outcome, you will be better for it. You will be better off, because you tried and gave it your best. You will come out on top. You are a winner, because you got out of your comfort zone and tried. You tried, because you have confidence in your ability to win and also because you have confidence in your ability to lose.

June 21

Affirmation: Today I will focus on how I am behaving on my journey.

This brings to mind how people act on the interstate, going twenty miles over the speed limit, cutting trucks off, not looking where they're going, and feeling entitled. What about the way people act on planes? People can be rude and impatient, talking on the cell phone, acting as if no one else is around, and not caring if anyone else is around. In bus stations people leave garbage behind, assuming that someone will clean it up. People leave places worse off than when they found them, because they're getting in their cars and not coming back.

Sometimes getting from point A to point B is pleasant. It depends upon how well you arrive at any destination. What does it mean to you to travel well? It means being prepared, having everything you need, not having excess baggage with you, and knowing where you are headed and what to expect when you arrive. Being well traveled is being polite, considerate, and kind. Patience and tolerance are vital. When do you feel that a pleasant journey is worth more than the destination?

June 22

Affirmation: I believe.

How can anyone dispute a belief in positive energy, that putting your best intentions out into the world or taking care of each other is a bad thing? What we give is what we get. The difficulty is in saying one thing and then doing another. The purpose of a daily intention is to make a conscious decision to work on areas that need work and to strengthen areas that are lacking. We know that being a good person is the way to be, and we know what that means, yet how many of us just can't quite get it right? We fall short. We get hurt. We may have been neglected or rejected. We might not know love. Do you currently have love in your life?

Some among us are bitter and have been put down so often they no longer see the purpose of getting out of bed. They find it almost impossible to live a life that matters.

I believe in goodness. I believe that people can change for the better, as easily as they can change for the worse. My daily prayer is that you receive the awareness it takes to make a difference. Make a positive difference in your life.

June 23

Affirmation: Today, when I feel down, I will get up!

Hurt, rejection and sadness all weigh heavy on our hearts, minds, bodies, and spirits at times—sadly for some more often than for others. It can be a chore to shake off feelings when other people don't understand you. When you are down and sadness is at your door, the mind plays tricks and makes it seemingly impossible to get up and get better. That's when you need a trusted friend to be your eyes and ears, someone you trust to be your advocate (your sponsor, so to speak) to help you get up and out of the slump you're in. You need a person to get you out of bed literally and figuratively. Sadness and depression run on a spectrum. Sometimes you need an objective person to help you through tough times. When you're unable to get up, ask for help. "Help!" Help is a four-letter word. So is love. That's it.

Help is available and will come if you are able to receive it. The reality is that when you're down, you're the last person to know it. When you're depressed or in the throes of unhealthy behavior, you think you don't need or want help. You think you can do this alone. You refuse intervention altogether. This is when your designated care person will be there for you to contact a minister, a doctor, or a mental health professional.

Don't stop when you are down. Try harder. Begin to realize, "Hey, I might be depressed." Eat right, get the right amount of sleep, exercise, and pray or meditate. Get help, and keep on going.

June 24

Affirmation: I want beauty in my life. I will be good.

How do you obtain and maintain beauty? Be good. Do well. Think good thoughts. Act out of love. That's it. You basically need nothing more, nothing less.

It's easy to be negative by putting yourself and others down. Our culture promotes judgment and criticism. Look at the reality shows. Everyone is fighting and flipping tables, trying to outdo the other guy. This type of culture actually promotes competition between friends and loved ones.

When you are feeling threatened by someone or even when you don't like what someone else is wearing, stop, think, breathe, and then act out of love. Don't be reactive in your thoughts, words, or actions. It's popular now to tell people, "I say what's on my mind, and if you don't like it that's too bad." This is not necessarily a good thing, and it doesn't help in your relationships or how you feel about yourself. Speaking your mind at all costs is rude, abrasive, and perhaps cruel. It promotes a bully generation.

Take a breath, and temper your dealings with people (and yourself) with love. Now look in the mirror. You are filled with beauty.

June 25

Affirmation: Today I will do one thing that scares me.

Some people come from two distinct perspectives in life. One is fear, and the other is love. When I ask people what they are afraid of, they look at me as if no one has ever asked them that question before. What are you afraid of? Is fear holding you back from something? It has the potential to keep you from being your authentic self. Fear is also anxiety producing. We are afraid of death and dying, bullies, and heights, among other phobias. Some people are even afraid of clowns. It's called coulrophobia.

Mainly we are afraid of ourselves, afraid of what we are capable of, and afraid of what we think we can't do. If you are fearful, ask yourself what it is that you're afraid of. Possibly what you fear most is contained to a very small area of your life. I suggest you do your thing despite your fear. Put what frightens you into perspective. Most fears are irrational.

Fears and phobias develop to protect you. They are no longer needed once you have gone through your trauma and have come out on the other side. If you still have work to do to eradicate fear, seek help. Living in fear is no way to live. Do one thing each day that scares you. Have fun.

June 26

Affirmation: Laughter is the best alternative medicine.

Laughter is a reaction to a commonality that is surprising, a universal concept that resonates with almost everyone. In other words, we laugh when something unexpected happens that we can relate to. When you are in the throes of a decision or life situation that has you paralyzed, take a moment to walk away. Think of something funny, ask a friend if he or she knows a good joke, and get out of your slump, if only for a moment. It can put your situation into perspective and allows you to "lighten up." Humor doesn't cost anything. It is a great tool in your quest to achieve or maintain balance in your life.

"Did you hear the one about ________________?"

June 27

Affirmation: Today I will remember only the good, not the bad.

A good memory recalls that which has created a positive foundation and a base for how we have gotten to this point in our lives. This comes in two ways: recognizing the good, affirming, happy, and healthy occurrence and events; and recognizing that even though we would not have intentionally chosen some of the negative times in our lives, the outcomes have helped to create who we are.

Hard times can develop strong qualities within us that might have otherwise remained dormant. These trials and tribulations can uncover talents and abilities that we never knew we possessed.

Do you remember the good things in your life, or are you the type of person who remembers only the bad and harbors resentment and anger? It is very common to have a hard time letting go of the times in your life when things didn't go well. Why? Because when things don't go your way or you are taken off guard by the way someone has offended you, or ruined your day, it hurts, and it is confusing at best. Perhaps you felt pain and experienced shame and anger. These feelings are extremely difficult to reconcile, and many of us repress the negative feelings until they surface at another time and place.

The people who have only good memories of the past are those who deal with hard times in the moment and then let go of the bad feelings and move on. They forgive and forget.

One way is not right or wrong. It is what you do with your feelings once time has passed that matters most. Letting go of animosity and refusing to harbor anger is a healthier, better path to take. In order to let go of the negativity of the past, first recognize that it's in the past and there is nothing you can do about it. Forgive the person who has harmed you even though he or she might not have apologized or been remorseful, and look to a happy future. Do it for yourself and those you love. Make it a habit, and make it a brighter future.

June 28

Affirmation: I will be at peace at home and away.

Patience and tolerance are vital when we leave the house each day and especially when we are away from home for extended periods of time. Why is it important to talk about our behavior while we are away? As a family therapist and mediator, I find that when families go on vacation, for example, what they want and expect to happen are often very different from what actually takes place. Perhaps couples go away and end up fighting. Families take vacations with extended family members or friends, and that also can be disastrous.

We take time off from work, leave the pressure of everyday life, and hope that for two weeks out of the year we can let go of animosity and stress and have fun. If you leave for vacation with a broken relationship or trouble at home, going away may intensify those feelings.

To prevent a meltdown when on vacation with family and friends, prepare to have downtime, and communicate with all members of your travel party. If someone wants to do something different, let that be okay. If someone is tired and wants to rest and not follow the crowd, respect that person's wishes. Remember—everyone is not on the same schedule, and everyone has different likes and dislikes. Perhaps a teenager is missing friends at home, for example. Talk things over, and listen to one another. You just might go home from vacation feeling rested and rejuvenated.

June 29

Affirmation: Today I will allow my feathers to get ruffled.

Are you a peacemaker at all costs? Do you not like being uncomfortable or upset? Do you not like it when your loved ones are upset for any reason? Are you the type of person who never *rocks the boat?* Sounds silly, but to be fully present and fully aware of our circumstances in life, we have to get upset every now ant then. It is normal!

Some people have had bad experiences with circumstances in their lives that they just don't want to face or even acknowledge. They pretend everything is fine and everyone around them is terrific. With blessings and love this is the case. But if you (or someone you love) are in denial or blind to what is happening around you, this just might be your wake up call. Listen to those who know and love you. Be all right (you don't have to be thrilled) with what they have to say. Try not to be defensive. Listen to what they are thinking and feeling: good, bad or indifferent. Keeping everything tied up in a neat, little package is a temporary fix. Open yourself up to new possibilities. It is okay to feel.

June 30

Affirmation: By virtue of the fact that I am human, I have the right to be happy.

Be honest with yourself. When was the last time that you simply and freely played without feeling self-conscious? I'm not talking about video games or surfing the Internet, but played, really played—did something simply for the joy and love of doing it?

The list of chores and things to do is long and never ending. There will always be something that haunts you, unfinished business, or a chore that you have been putting off. The items on your to-do list can vary in volume—from whispering to shouting at you—but in spite of all the duties and responsibilities that are in the background or forefront of our minds, when was the last time you gave yourself permission to do something decadent, luxurious, and fun, like playing? Again, this is not about mindlessly passing time, but getting lost in having fun.

Remember the last time that you forgot about yourself and your troubles for a moment and had fun doing something that filled your heart, fed your soul, and helped you to focus on the joy of being fully present and alive while doing something you liked to do. Take time to play. Make time to play. "I am too busy" is an excuse. There is time, and it's time now to plan to play!

July

National Picnic Month

July 1

Affirmation: Generosity is a divine gift.

The best thing to do if you're feeling poor is to give something away. Give a few dollars to a homeless person, donate some clothes to a thrift shop. Instead of focusing on what you don't have, focus on what you do have and how you can bless others with it. Being able to give is a divine gift.

It is not up to you to determine others' needs. If you choose to give only to those who appear to be in need on the outside, you are discounting those who may have everything but have not felt human kindness or have not felt love or appreciation in a very long time, if ever.

I am spiritually blessed. My family and I provide shelter, food, and buying power together. Our need for love, kindness, and understanding is satisfied. Collectively, we need or want for nothing.

My good fortune would not be possible if it was not for the help and assistance of extended family and friends. Grandma and Grandpa were there for our children. Siblings, aunts, uncles, cousins, nieces, and nephews by the dozens living all over the world make up our family and delight and surprise us daily. Friends and our community bring the laughter and the fun. "Want to get together for a picnic?" *All right.* "Need something? I'll be right over."

Everyone you are with is an angel in disguise. Your blessings of love, kindness, and understanding are what make you rich.

July 2

Affirmation: I will let go and let God in meditation and prayer.

Prayer is the way we connect to energy, the guiding light that holds the future. Some people have a hard time with the concept of prayer. The only reason I can think of is that they associate prayer with religion. Not a fan of religion? Don't like prayer? In your youth you learned rote prayers that may or may not have made sense to you. If this has stopped you from praying, break out and come up with your own—whatever works for you. No one is judging you anymore.

Let's take a look at what the purpose of prayer is. Prayer seeks to establish or reestablish connection with a spiritual entity through talking or listening. You pray to worship, to request help, to confess, or to express your thoughts and emotions. You pray for yourself or your loved ones. Prayer or meditation may be practiced by anyone at any time.

The goal of meditation is to induce a state of awareness to clear the mind and ease many health issues, such as high blood pressure, headaches, and fatigue. Meditation is designed to promote relaxation, to build internal energy, and to develop compassion, love, patience, generosity, and forgiveness. Meditation attempts to rid the body, mind, and spirit of negativity, such as anger and hatred. It promotes kind awareness and other loving emotions. Meditation has a calming effect and directs awareness inward until a calm and relaxed feeling is achieved.

July 3

Affirmation: Today I will set my soul free.

The soul is defined as the mortal essence of a living thing. According to the *Merriam-Webster Dictionary*, the soul is "the spiritual principle in human beings; a person's total self." It is the moral and emotional nature of human beings. The quality that arouses emotion and sentiment and spiritual or moral force is known as the soul. Are you in touch with your soul and spirituality? Do you ever think of the essence of who you are? Can you explain the energy that makes you who you are?

You are in touch with your soul when you step outside of your thoughts. You are in touch with your soul when emotions are released and you feel at peace. You are in your soulful space when you are sitting on a beach or experiencing nature and feeling happiness and pure joy. You feel empowered. You feel renewed and refreshed, as if the cares and responsibilities that have encompassed you for so long no longer matter. When you are in touch with your soul, your body and mind are in harmony. Never forget and never neglect your soulfulness.

July 4

Affirmation: Today I will be self-reliant.

The opposite of self-reliance is reliance and dependency on others. We all need other people in our lives. But to what degree do we use them for that which we are capable of doing ourselves? Getting a book down from a shelf comes to mind. Asking for help is fine if you can't reach and there is no ladder around.

It is common to become dependent on others for our happiness. It is also common to be dependent on others for our misery. "If you would just stop doing this or start that." "I'm unhappy in my relationship because of what my partner is or isn't doing."

Here is the wake-up call. No one can make you feel bad unless you allow someone to do so. In other words, how you choose to react to the slings and arrows of others is up to you. Your happiness depends on your actions and reactions, not those of another person. This is your life. Self-reliance commands your participation in how your book turns out. You can be dependent on others or independent, but the balance is interdependence. Interdependence is having healthy, positive relationships in your life, by choice. The people in your life make you better. You enhance each other's lives. Today let's celebrate Interdependence Day!

July 5

Affirmation: Today I will break away from negativity.

Take a moment—right here, right now—and make a list of the things that you consciously view negatively. Think of the people about whom you have bad thoughts. Think of the negative messages you send to yourself on a daily basis. Then ask yourself, "Why?" Why are you judgmental of yourself and others? Do you think somehow it makes you feel better? How's that working for you?

When someone makes you feel incompetent in any way, move on. That person doesn't have your best interest at heart. For that matter, ask yourself if you have your best interest at heart. Negativity is insidious. When people are critical, you may turn around and criticize others. If someone is judgmental about you, you may tend to be judgmental about others. Give it up; it doesn't do anyone any good. Only bad situations and hurt feelings come from putting people down.

July 6

Affirmation: Today I will give myself a break.

You are your own worst critic. You are hardest on yourself. You are the only one stressing yourself out. What we all need is to be nicer to ourselves. Allow yourself a little extra sleep. Take a long, hot bath. Take a break from alcohol or sugar. Pray or meditate. Refresh and rejuvenate. You may not think that you're the cause of your stress, but you are. Think about it. Who is ultimately responsible for the choices you make? You are. And who is responsible for the situation you are in, good or bad? Recognize that you have options. You only see the options life presents when you take the time to be in a calm and relaxed state. Many can't remember the last time they were calm and relaxed, but that thinking is self-imposed. We are the way we are because of our choices. Consider the alternative—avoiding a negative impact on your health and relationships. If you are where you want to be, living your authentic life, teach and show others how it's done.

July 7

Affirmation: Today I will not be confined by my self-imposed limitations.

When it comes down to it, some of our limitations are self-imposed. There is an abundance of limitations that are not within our control, such as physical, genetic, intellectual, financial, cultural, familial, political, and legal limitations, to name a few. The list goes on. Of course, there are exceptions. Most folks limit themselves. Are you unwilling or unable? Do you hesitate out of fear? Do you let past experiences cloud your judgment? What would you do if you had no fear? If you're in the right place and are prepared and ready, there is nothing stopping you but yourself and your preconceived notions that things won't work out. They might not. But then again they might, and this is the essence of achievement and living the life you were intended to live. You can now let go of your fear.

July 8

Affirmation: I am the master of my fate.

To what causes are you devoted? To what have you dedicated your life? "Devotion" is a beautiful word. To be devoted is to be loyal and lovingly committed to something or someone.

What have you mastered so far in life? Do you currently have something that you're working on mastering? Perhaps there's something you've considered and you are beginning to think that now might be a good time to start.

Become the master of your fate. Master your own destiny. Having something to strive for fosters healthy self-esteem and happiness. Mastering a talent can be the truest form of knowing who you are and what you stand for. Have a plan for your life; envision it, desire it, and go for it. Mastering takes devotion to something about which you are passionate.

July 9

Affirmation: I am the strongest when I need to be.

Life is hard. You can't deny the struggles you face. Every day there is a tragedy somewhere in the world, possibly in your own backyard. You don't like to think about the hard times you've faced. You may be in denial. The hard times you must endure can be overwhelming and unmanageable. You may find yourself stuck and find it difficult to enjoy life.

Where are you in your life? Are you in a good place? Have the difficult times in your life defined you, or have they made you stronger? When hard times hit, it can be crippling to work through the pain, grief, fear, and trauma. What's essential to living a purposeful life is taking these moments and using them to make life meaningful despite what you're going through. You are called on to dig deep and find out what you're made of.

Be proud of your resilience, your capabilities, and the resolve that you might not even know you have. When thinking of the hard times you've had, be thankful you survived and thankful that you're a better person for them.

July 10

Affirmation: Let go, and let God.

Of all the affirmations in this little book, "Let go, and let God" is the most powerful one for me. It speaks of faith, trust, surrendering, and letting go of the need to be in control and to always be right. People who think they need to be in control of everything and everyone are usually the most unfulfilled and unhappy. Those who no longer trust and lack faith in themselves, others, and their God are possibly living a life of conflict and strife. The need to control everything can lead to power struggles that can be endless and destructive.

What does it mean to let go and let God? See this short but powerful phrase as prayer. Say the prayer, and then take a step back, meditate, and reflect. Let go of all thoughts surrounding your current situation for now. You will soon see results. What you're doing is taking your ego out of the equation. You're letting go of the drama.

The world won't fall apart. Tasks will get done. The end result might just fool you. The results may be better than what you could have come up with by worrying and obsessing. The results just might be God inspired.

July 11

Affirmation: Today I will spend time with God, because I need a shot of strength.

When you are at your lowest point, when you are tired, weary, and emotionally distraught, it's hard to remember to call on God. However, this is the time you need God most. When you're down, you are preoccupied with your struggles and you worry. You don't like the way your situation is going, and chances are you don't like the way you are handling or reacting to the situation either. When you're down, you might seek the counsel of a loved one or a friend. When the people in your life don't give you the answers you are looking for or do not side with you, your feelings are hurt, and you feel sad and angry. You feel alone.

Now is the time to go for a walk. Get out of your head. Your head is not a good place in which to hang out. Take a break, and meditate. Say a prayer, and feel lighter. Your spirit will lift, and you'll feel revived. Give prayer a chance.

July 12

Affirmation: Today I will wait patiently for the answers to my questions.

Is it all right to be confused? Some say it means you're paying attention. The world is confusing, and many people choose to shut down. They are not paying attention to what is going on around them. I believe the state of confusion for most of us can be a catalyst to creating balance in life. When we are not certain what is the right course of action, when we don't know where we are headed, and when we doubt ourselves, we end up in a place where something has to give.

Confusion is very insidious. It is not easily recognizable. Many people think this or that is wrong with them when, in fact, they are confused. Once you realize that life's questions can be tackled without fatal consequences, all is well, and the healing process begins. So what is confusion, really?

Being confused is lacking understanding or being uncertain or unclear in one's mind about something. It stands to reason that if you are unclear about whatever it may be that is troubling you, at any given moment you tend to get anxious and fearful and shut down. A healthy mind seeks out answers, but when you don't have all the answers you have basically two options: seek the answers to your questions and educate yourself until you feel satisfied and your confusion is abated; or patiently wait.

Patiently waiting is not the same as shutting down or repressing thoughts. Patiently waiting takes skill. Patience also takes faith in yourself, the people around you, and the universe. It will all be made known to us through healthy measures. Walk, meditate, eat right, rest, and talk it out. Confusion lifts until the next time. And when the next time comes along, you will be that much better at recognizing "There's nothing wrong with me. I'm just confused."

July 13

Affirmation: I am better for it.

Look at the people around you. Are they friends or strangers? Think about each one individually. Imagine the people in your life. Perhaps they're family members, colleagues, or neighbors. Now think of what they have gone through in their lives. Do you know? Are they survivors, defeatists, or champions? You might not know what other people have gone through in their lives. You may not have the slightest idea about their childhood or their early years. You may not even be aware of their current struggles. People are in our lives to help us and to teach us through their stories, if we are open to them.

What others have gone through will often surprise or perhaps shock you. We've all had a multitude of life crises and experiences. Imagine the most successful person you know, one who you truly admire. Are you aware of the heartache, pain, and suffering he or she has endured, or the triumphs and pinnacles of his or her life? It's probably a pretty amazing story.

Be the author of your own story. The pain and suffering you are called upon to bear is unique to you. Emerge triumphantly, with as many scars as possible, so you can go on to help others. It feels good to have something good come from our adversity.

July 14

Affirmation: I pray for strength.

What would an easy life be like? Life can be fun and amazing with twists and turns, but it's never easy. Perhaps you pray to have your burden lifted. It's natural to want the pain to go away and the hard times to be over. You have spent countless hours contemplating why life is so hard. But it just is! There is no rhyme or reason. Life is difficult. Period.

Now when you ask for guidance, help, and support, make sure you throw in strength. Are you strong enough to handle what life sends your way? Can you be strong enough to be there for your family when they need you? Of course you can. You have no choice. You have what it takes. You have faith.

July 15

Affirmation: I am gentle. I am strong. I am loved.

In order to truly love yourself or others, you have to be gentle. Morally weak people are cruel. They prey on others. The bully picks on the one who is seemingly weak and unable to stand up for himself or herself. It makes the bully feel better to make his or her target feel bad. The thing about bullies is that they don't choose their victims randomly.

Were you bullied as a child, or are you being bullied now? Recognize that bullies are weak. They have been hurt, and they have yet to develop the skills it takes to rise above the hurt. They stay stuck in their hurt and confusion. Should you pity or feel sorry for a bully? That's up to you. Try not to be in the position of being an easy target. Where do you fall on the spectrum? Can you teach others the importance of standing up for themselves in a loving and kind way?

It is common to think that the victim is weak and the offender is strong. It's actually the exact opposite. The bully is weak, and those who survive the attack or the injustice are much stronger for it. Be gentle. Be strong. Be yourself.

July 16

Affirmation: I am working on a better me.

Are you just starting to understand, or have you already realized, that you are, in fact, the master of your own destiny? The truth is that we cannot blame others for our mistakes. We cannot expect friends and loved ones to make up our minds for us. You are it. You make decisions that are amazing, and you take the spotlight. When you make disastrous decisions, you experience failure. It is imperative to recognize that every decision you make can be altered. You can turn a bad situation around. Many people make poor choices and make the decision to live with that bad choice. Please don't be a victim of your own life. Regain your power. You, and only you, are the master of your life.

July 17

Affirmation: Keep trying. Keep going. Don't quit.

Continuous effort is the key to unlocking your potential. This means that if you keep at it, you will amaze yourself with your hidden talents. You have amazed yourself on more than one occasion. Whether it was a delicious dish you made for dinner or a discovery you made in your chosen profession, just when you thought the situation was over your head, you kept going. If it is something about which you are passionate, there is no stopping the creativity, mastery, and genius inside you. We all have untapped potential, hidden talents that are waiting to come forth and amaze. What is it that you are willing to continue doing? Go for it, and keep it up.

July 18

Affirmation: In service I can add caring and kindness.

When I call a company for assistance, it is frustrating at best to talk to a representative who will not answer your question, gives you off to someone else, or basically tells you that there is nothing they can do to help. Why can't that person take a breath and give it that extra effort and say, "Let me look," or "I'll ask someone and see what I can do."

Providing service means taking care of each other, caring enough to provide what the other person needs or wants. That's it, pure and simple. The basic concept of caring is lost on some people. I have heard a thousand times that our youth do not care. Maybe it's because we collectively have taught them not to care. I know many young adults who are driven to make a difference, to seek out those in need, to run marathons, to have car washes, and to raise funds and awareness for others. Look at the ALS Ice Bucket Challenge of 2014. The result was getting people to care and to raise money and awareness for a cause that might not be as visual as others. Let's teach caring and kindness to others by continuing to lead by example.

July 19

Affirmation: Today I will take care of myself. I will eat right, exercise, and get enough sleep.

You overreact when you are in a not-so-great place. Whether it is body, mind, or spirit, something has to give when we are out of balance. Why is it so important for us to stay in balance?

When you are ill, in pain, tired, or out of shape, your needs are greater than what you have to offer others. Your resistance and resilience can become compromised. Don't let them. When you are in shape and in a good place in body, mind, and spirit, you have extra to give. You have extra time, energy, and a willingness to help. You are the giver. You can share your love, joy, and optimism.

Being the calm amid the chaos can happen only when you are coming from a positive place, where you can be rational and solid and give of yourself in a productive way rather than making the situation worse. If you can't be the calm, step back and let someone else lead. Nothing is worse than being in the way and not helping the situation. Level heads will prevail. Trust that things will work out. Everything will work out as it is meant to be.

July 20

Affirmation: Today, when the storm comes, I will rise above the drama.

Running from your problems is never a good thing. Situations will keep coming back again and again until you finally deal with what's going on. Hiding or avoiding the situation altogether just makes you weak and afraid.

The eagle is always prepared. It knows what to do. When hard times come, it does what it has always done. It rises above. If you've ever taken the path of the eagle and risen above, you know how good it feels not to be swept up. The eagle never has to stop and think. It always knows what to do ahead of time. It's always ready.

Prepare yourself spiritually and emotionally for the next storm to come. Don't be caught not knowing what to do. Take the high road. Fly like an eagle.

July 21

Affirmation: I will be thoughtful with my words.

It is sad how couples sometimes speak to each other with demeaning tones, distaining gestures, and disparaging words. Parents speak to their children with disrespect and anger. Friends and family talk disrespectfully via the phone, text, e-mail, or social media. The messages and chats often center on words and attitudes that are critical, sniping, sarcastic, and often untrue. You think that putting someone down can make you feel better about yourself. You think you just have to get it out no matter what you say or how it makes someone else feel.

There are people who seem to get joy out of critiquing and complaining. They often temper their tones with a know-it-all attitude. Complaining and being negative are second nature. Beyond being downright nasty, how is this helpful to anyone in the long run? If you tell your friends what you think no matter how hurtful those comments are, chances are the people in your life will stoop to your level. Rise above, and be someone who builds up rather than tears down.

July 22

Affirmation: I don't need evidence that God exists.

God exists within me. That's all I know. Carl Sagan wrote frequently about religion and the relationship between religion and science. He expressed his skepticism about the conventional conceptualization of God as a sapient being. He continues to say that if, by God, one means the set of physical laws that govern the universe, then clearly there is such a God.

On atheism, Sagan commented, "An atheist is someone who is certain that God does not exist, someone who has compelling evidence against the existence of God. I know of no such compelling evidence. We would have to know a great deal more about the universe than we do now to be sure that no such God exists." He did not agree that there is a God, and he did not adhere to stating there is no God. There you have it.

Regarding the relationship between religion and science, Carl Sagan stated, "Science is not only compatible with spirituality; it is a profound source of spirituality. When we recognize our place in an immensity of light-years and in the passage of ages, when we grasp the intricacy, beauty, and subtlety of life, then that soaring feeling, that sense of elation and humility combined, is surely spiritual."

July 23

Affirmation: I recognize the importance of the pause.

Our intention lies in the breath between the spoken words. Be still. Find a place that is quiet. Breathe in and out deeply and purposefully. Your intentions lie within the space between your breath and the words you speak. Quiet your mind. The simple act of being aware of your breathing calms the soul and connects you to your spirit.

The power of taking a moment to pause can work for all of us in all our daily interactions. I see many people who don't take time out at work for a coffee break or who eat lunch at their desks. They can't stop what they're doing long enough to eat! That sounds crazy, doesn't it? What's crazy is that our society is so overworked and underpaid. I suggest you get up and walk away for a breather every now and then or take time to have a meal away from the office. Take lunch at a nearby park perhaps. I suggest that interval breaks and time away from work during the day are essential to healthy and happy workers. The power of the pause promotes progress and success in working relationships with self and with others.

July 24

Affirmation: Today I will take a moment to pause before I react.

"That which does not kill us makes us stronger" is a catchphrase that has recently gained momentum. Why? Because it resonates with mostly everyone.

When someone is hurting, your natural tendency is to go to him or her and try to help. It's sometimes hard to find just the right thing to say, so you lead with "What doesn't kill you makes you stronger." Sometimes it helps. Sometimes it seems disingenuous. It minimizes or trivializes what the person is going through.

So what can you do? Have you ever thought that perhaps Feiedrich Nietzsche, the nineteenth century German philosopher who is responsible for this quote was working out his own troubles and struggles with this iconic catchphrase? Most of what we say and do is for our own purposes. If this was not a personal revelation for him, it would not have occurred to him. So when you find yourself giving other people advice, recognize that the advice you are handing out is not only for the person for whom you intend it; it's also advice you could use yourself. It is advice you have needed firsthand. Every now and then think about the advice you are dishing out. Is it what you need to be listening to yourself? Maybe. Maybe not. Whatever you do, think about the person and what he or she might be going through. Keep your responses specifically geared toward that person. What you say will help if it is what that person needs to hear, not something you need to say. Temper your words with kindness and love.

July 25

Affirmation: I am patient.

What will it take to get through this crisis? Time. What heals all wounds? Time. How much time? Are you patient enough to wait? Not always. No one who is in trouble or trauma can see what lies ahead. How much time does it take to mend a broken heart? How much time does it take to realize your dreams? Seriously, how much time does it take?

I find that most major life changes—change in marital status, relocation, a new job, a loss, or a breakup—can take up to two full years to adjust to. Some require more time, some less. The first stage in adjusting to a new situation involves changing thoughts, actions, patterns, and behaviors. The second stage involves adaptation and acceptance. Move on, and move forward. Time can be a healer. Take the time to experience the process of positive change and growth in your life. Have fun while practicing patience.

July 26

Affirmation: Heaven is where I am.

Self-love and self-awareness are necessary to fuel positive emotions. Love yourself, be kind and positive, and you can get through almost anything life has to offer, whether you know it or not. Live one day at a time. Be in the present, and follow your path. Be well. Know peace, and let the rest go. This is your gift to yourself and to others. Your wisdom is to be honored. Let your spirit guide you. Allow yourself to experience heaven on earth.

What does that mean? It means that you allow your source, your positive energy, into your heart to work for good and happiness. Hope is within all of us. Hope is when you know in your heart and mind that the future will be as it should be and that everything will be fine. Grace and wisdom are yours. Tap into the wisdom you have accumulated throughout the years through trial and error. What you know for sure is valuable and should be showcased. Never underestimate yourself or your experiences. Even tears and fear will not keep you from where you need to be. I know that you will make it.

July 27

Affirmation: Taking time to have fun is good.

When you were a child, you were all about fun. After a while, parents, teachers, and adults in general began to tell you to stop having fun and be serious, to stop talking and pay attention. Fun was for later. Then later came, and you forgot how to have fun. Having fun was squashed into what others expected of you. You have now given up on joy. Sound familiar?

It's important for adults to go back to having fun. The message is basic and simple. It is universal and timeless.

Laughter is the best medicine. Do not take yourself too seriously. Make an opportunity to fly a kite or throw a snowball. Trust me—more than likely you will not poke your eye out!

July 28

Affirmation: Today, when I encounter art (and I will) I will appreciate the beauty in life.

Walking into a building or someone's home, we see pictures hanging on the wall and walk right by. We see photos in books and skim past them. On the Internet we see beautiful posts with lovely colors or hear music that someone has composed but quickly turn it off or down out of habit. I encourage you today to stop and give that artwork a moment of your undivided attention. Give a thought to why the painting is there. What was the artist thinking? What do you like or don't like about the piece? All these thoughts take under thirty seconds.

We were told as children to hurry up and get to where we were going. I suggest you slow down. The signs you are looking for in life are all around you in the beauty that you encounter. I suggest art is everywhere to pique your curiosity, stimulate a feeling, get you out of your comfort zone, and beg you to expand your thoughts, feelings, and experiences. Art is there to expand your horizons. It might not be the first painting or song you encounter, but it is perhaps something that strikes you or causes you to pause. Is it a drawing of a landscape or an abstract oil painting or a sculpture outside of the local library? Is there a genre that you are interested in but haven't pursued because you have been too busy and didn't have the time or money to enjoy? Look for something artistic that speaks to you. Be on the lookout. Oh, and while your at it, help a starving artist; buy art!

July 29

Affirmation: Today I will turn my negativity around.

It is very difficult, at best, to say that we have control over our emotions, but in the end we do. We tend to blame people, places, or things for causing us to feel a certain way. Your job, your family, or the house you grew up in can trigger joy, sadness, anger, elation, pride, fear, shame, and so on. Triggers do not cause feelings; they either contribute to or contaminate our happiness, pain, or suffering. We have control of how we think, feel, and act. Thinking otherwise is playing the blame game.

If you think and act happy, forgive, and not blame, your mood will improve. Of course, no one disputes that. If you think negatively and act badly, consider changing the way you look at things. You can always turn your situation around to better reflect who and what you are authentically. For today, surround yourself with people who are uplifting and try looking at things from a more positive perspective. It can't hurt.

July 30

Affirmation: The kindest hearts have felt the most pain.

The reason you have a pretty smile, the prettiest eyes, and the kindest heart is that you allow yourself to cry and feel pain. Deal with your sorrow, and then do what you have to do to move on.

Sometimes we don't handle our emotions in a healthy way. We don't want to confront our feelings; instead we push them down deep inside. This is called repression, and many suffer from it. It's easier not to deal with your feelings than to take a hard, realistic look at what is going on with you at any given time. What can you do if you're not dealing with what's going on in your life? Try releasing the stress and anxiety that are toxic. If you want to feel beautiful and look amazing, try letting go of whatever it is that is bothering you. Talk about it with a friend, work it out in the gym, or talk to a professional. Love life, and give love to others. Share your experiences, good or bad. Learn, and grow into the beautiful person you are meant to be.

July 31

Affirmation: I am good enough.

Never think that you are not good enough. By now you have heard that you should like yourself. You must have a sense of who you are and what you like. It's okay to be you. That may be all well and good, but the difficulty lies in actually thinking, feeling, and acting as if you are good enough. Many of us are in a constant battle with our emotions. Perhaps you were taught to think of yourself as less than or not worthy of love, praise, or even kindness. Perhaps you were taught as a small child that if you were praised too much, you would become conceited. If that sounds familiar to you, you have your work cut out for you. The good news is it is never too late to shake off the negativity of your past and change your way of thinking about yourself.

If you're feeling inadequate and unappreciated by those closest to you, it may be a hard road ahead to break away and to break out. Refuse to accept the cruel treatment of others toward you. Develop clear and consistent boundaries. The critics in your inner circle who constantly tear you down have to stop. They will stop when you no longer allow them to hurt you. They will have to move on to someone else. You can be bullied at any age. Recognize it as such, and do something about it. Refuse to be teased, put down, or demeaned. You are worth so much more.

August

Happiness Happens Month

August 1

Affirmation: Life is a joy filled with delightful surprises.

You can choose joy. You always have a choice—not necessarily in what comes your way or how it does, but you can choose how to respond. You can choose to be joyful. You can choose to not let negativity bring you down. You can rise above your circumstances. True joy is the calm amidst the storm.

When you are in a bad mood, feeling down, or experiencing anger at the world, look for the positive in any given situation. Be the one who remains positive and optimistic. It can make the difference in how you ultimately solve the problem and how you resolve issues in the future.

How can you choose to be joyful when you are distraught? By choosing not to be hateful or vindictive. When you are upset, recognize it as such, and confront the issues at hand. Talk it out. When you have complaints about someone or something, or you are feeling neglected or misunderstood, choose not to hold onto the bad feelings. Instead of creating a firestorm, recognize that you are angry; it will pass if you choose to let it go. If you hang onto the suffering, it will keep you from who you are meant to be—a kind, loving, and caring person who doesn't want to stay down for long.

August 2

Affirmation: I will not let other people define who I am.

It takes time and courage to develop your own personal style. It is daunting to decide who you are and what you want to be. It's not easy to be authentic. It requires strength of character. When you live out who you are, you are subject to criticism. Don't be afraid; people will like you.

When you're young, it can be scary not to be liked by the other kids. Anyone who stands out is subject to ridicule. At some point in your life you must make a decision to go with the crowd or be your own person. Are you the one who broke out and did your own thing, or are you the one still trying to fit in? Either way it's never easy. Being true to yourself might not be easy, but it is always preferable. It's emotionally draining to live the way you think others want you to live.

I advocate for being you. Each day is an opportunity to get in touch with what brings you joy and what makes you happy. If you want to be creative in your style of dress, be your unique self. If you're the only one laughing at a joke, good for you. At least you're laughing. Pray, eat, and laugh the way that works for you.

August 3

Affirmation: Today I will take the scenic way home.

Don't always walk the straight and narrow road. The path of least resistance leads to nowhere. Get on a highway that takes you up hills, over rivers, and over mountains to the sea. This is God's country. When you have pen in hand, make swirls, circles, and squiggly lines instead of lines drawn in the sand. Let your creative mind take you where the designs that you make are awe inspired. When you travel through the cycles of life, change your direction and don't be afraid to go around the block a few times. Curves aren't bumps. Curves give shape and beauty to life.

August 4

Affirmation: When I feel down, I know I have a friend.

Friends make you laugh. They know you, and they know your sense of humor. They say things that no one else would say—good or bad, helpful or hurtful. A friend gives you room to be yourself. If you want to jump up and sing a Broadway show tune, go right ahead. If while playing charades you act like a total fool, great! Friends laugh with you and cry with you.

Friends know what you mean when other people don't. They might not agree with you, but chances are they understand you. This might be all you'll ever need from a friend. True friends cherish the good times. Bad times, hopefully, are cast into the wind.

In my life, I have received friendship from countless amazing people. In return I try to be a true friend. I have learned that the only way to have a friend is to be a friend. Be the one to pick up the phone and make that call. Be the one who apologizes first. That is what friends do. If you keep the lines of communication open, you will find that your friend will still be there for you when you least expect it yet need him or her the most. I am keenly aware of the joy and happiness friendships provide. I have a strong feeling today I will reach out to a friend. Friends make life much easier and a lot more fun.

August 5

Affirmation: Today I will giggle for no apparent reason.

Laughter is the best medicine. Humor can be an antidote for a moment of feeling down. Who are the people in your life who make you laugh? They know you, and they get you. People who make you laugh see a commonality in life, and they know that they can "go there" with you and you won't take offense. Or if you do take offense, there is cause to pause and adjust.

Humor is the element of surprise. When we feel helpless and hopeless we see the world as one dimensional, one-note. Predictable. When you laugh it's because you didn't expect that. Predictability isn't funny. Making someone laugh is saying something that others were thinking but didn't have the nerve to say. My beloved mother taught me to always have a joke ready to cheer someone up. Tell a joke to cheer yourself up. Don't be afraid to make fun of yourself and do something silly or totally ridiculous. You will be sure to brighten someone's day.

August 6

Affirmation: The truth about me is ________________________.

If someone were to write your life story, would you allow him or her to tell everything or just a highly edited version? Is your life an open book, or do you keep secrets that weigh you down?

It's a good exercise to write your story down on paper—not for anyone else to see perhaps, but for you to see how everything you've gone through so far affects your life today. It's also healthy to dig down deep and take a look at the memories you might have repressed. It could turn out that what you thought you couldn't revisit, you can and that it feels good to let your emotions out and let them go. Your past can perhaps shed light on your current situation. Your memories might not have the strong grip on you now that you thought they did. Take yourself back in time—go way back to your childhood—and dig deep. Assess your life, then assess your life now, and move on. Your inner child wants you to visit every now and then.

August 7

Affirmation: When I feel hate building up inside me, I will think of what it is that I love.

Do you experience hatred? Be honest. It is probably one of the most difficult emotions to let go of. Think about the times in your life when you felt hatred toward either someone specific or others you may not even know. Think of a circumstance, an organization, or even a moment of self-hatred. Perhaps you are harboring hatred at this moment.

Self-hatred is learned. It can be reversed. Self-hatred stems from low self-esteem and degradation. Talk it out. Do what you need to do, and accomplish new goals. If you make choices that promote you moving in a positive direction, your achievements will lead to appreciating yourself and working toward a place of accomplishment. Stop telling yourself that you are less than, and start telling yourself that you are good enough. You don't have to go from zero to sixty. Start with "I am a good-enough friend," for example. "I am good enough." Then you can take it steps further to "I love myself, and I am great." Pray or meditate about it, and let conquering self-hatred be your goal.

August 8

Affirmation: I listen to my favorite music to calm down or to rev up!

Research shows that you can boost your mood by listening to music. Your favorite song can also restore energy and even help the body heal naturally. I feel invigorated when I listen to music in the car. I listen to music while doing chores. Listening to the lyrics and the melody takes me out of the moment. Songs that are universal speak to a moment in our lives or a feeling we want to have at that particular moment. Songs speak to us, literally. Music says what we are thinking but cannot put into words. When we have questions, a song on the radio tells us it will be all right.

Brilliant music is the crown of comfort, virtue, and holiness. It brings soul to an otherwise barren landscape. Music provides peace of mind, propels the imagination to soar, and brings happiness to life and wherever else our imaginations take us. Music allows us to be silent and calm. Music is healing. Music is universal. Everyone loves music.

August 9

Affirmation: All we have is now.

What does it mean to be truly in the moment and to live in the now? Being present is a concept that is new to the Western culture. People who are stuck in the past are rarely open to change. Living in the past protects some people from experiencing the pain and sorrow they associate with living outside of their comfort zone. Living in the past prevents us from moving forward and living a balanced and connected life. On the other hand, worrying about the future is a complete waste of time. I say "worry" because planning for the future is constructive, but living your life with a what-if mentality prevents us from living our authentic lives.

So how do you live in the moment? Catch yourself when your thoughts are stuck for too long in either the past or the future. Bring yourself to what it is you are doing at the moment or whom you are talking with. Focus on the task at hand. When you are in a moment of silence and contemplation, rid your mind of all thoughts. Just allow yourself to be in the moment of peace and solitude. Now move on to live your best life in the here and now.

August 10

Affirmation: I am proud of my age. It suits me.

How old are you? It is not a trick question. People are funny about their age. It begins in childhood. We want to be older than we are. We want to be teenagers, then we want to be adults, and then when we turn a certain age we want to reverse the hands of time.

Billions of dollars are spent on trying to get this nation to look younger. Who cares? You are what you are.

Be the best you can be no matter how many candles are on your birthday cake. Celebrate your life in terms of success, love, and joy rather than numbers. Your age is amazing. It is one thing that you have no control over. Embrace your life, and be loud and proud about how old (or young) you are.

August 11

Affirmation: Today I will fail better.

Have you ever heard the expression "Failing is not an option"? That's one thing that I don't believe I've ever said. Perhaps I'm a realist. Whenever you set out to do something, the chance of failure is very real. There are factors in life that are outside of your control and that you have not planned on.

When you fail, you learn so that you will not repeat your mistakes. *I'm not going to do that again.* Failure is simply not doing what you set out to do. Get over it. Winning brings on an element of happiness, a high. Failure produces disappointment and discouragement. These opposite emotions are fleeting and do not need to stay with you forever.

August 12

Affirmation: If I can't be sincere, I'll be quiet.

Sincerity is being honest and heartfelt with your feelings, thoughts, and desires. Virtue is speaking and acting truly about your feelings, thoughts, and desires. I believe you have moments of insincerity, but for the most part you are sincere. Perhaps you act sweetly and pleasantly when people really want to strangle you. This could be at work or at the shopping mall. At the mechanic's shop or in the doctor's office, do you speak and act honestly? Try it. Be authentic. This doesn't mean you can act out and be a lunatic. You can, however, say what you are feeling and be sad if that is how you are feeling in the moment. Don't repress or hide your feelings. If you feel you can't be real at the moment, then come back when you are better able to handle the situation. Pretending you are in a place that you are not, from time to time, is necessary, but don't make it a habit. It's not healthy. It's physically, mentally, and emotionally draining. Try telling someone the truth when he or she asks you how you are. It might feel funny at first, but in the long run you will feel lighter if your burden is lifted, if for only that moment.

August 13

Affirmation: Today I will be kind to others and to myself.

How often during the day do you find yourself treating people badly or being just plain nasty—being dismissive or impatient with others at the grocery store, talking about a friend behind that person's back, or yelling at or being short-tempered with a child? Feeling lonely, neglected, or unappreciated is normal. At times, we find ourselves taking our hostility out on others. Hopefully, this type of behavior is not a conscious decision. You can turn your negative reactions around.

Now that you know this is happening, you can do something about it. Don't allow yourself to lose control of your emotions. Take care of yourself physically. Exercise, and eat right. Get enough sleep. Talk out your problems, and don't let them build up. Be proactive, and do what you need to do to always live a balanced life.

August 14

Affirmation: I will live my life with a kind, loving and genuine spirit.

Why is it that you can be one way one moment and then completely the opposite the next moment? We are walking contradictions. We talk about walking our walk and talking our talk, but that is impossible all the time. Many people are overly outgoing at parties but will tell you they are really very shy. I believe this is a way of overcompensating. They don't want to feel the pain of their shyness, so they work really hard on being outgoing. That can be very painful and emotionally exhausting. Rather, be at peace with the fact that you are shy in some areas and work on yourself slowly and purposefully. This goes for any weakness you might feel is holding you back. Perhaps you talk too much out of anxiety or fail to live life to the fullest because you are afraid to succeed. Give yourself a pass. Allow yourself a much need dose of self-encouragement. Give yourself permission to take life one step at a time, one day at a time. Live authentically with a kind and loving spirit.

August 15

Affirmation: Smiling at someone just might turn his or her day around.

Smile. People will wonder what you're up to. When you smile from the heart, mind, and spirit, you are in a good place.

Nothing is bothering you, and you are not feeling any stress. Did you ever think that smiling when you are not in a good place would lift your spirits? Of course you have. If this is proven, then why don't more people smile? Is it because they are too deep in thought or too busy thinking about things they don't want to be thinking about? Is it because they are hurting, angry, or lonely? Every now and then, I find myself frowning or not having any expression at all. It is then that I become aware and smile even though I know no one is watching. It's a little experiment I do. Now when I am with others, I smile and hope that it can have a positive effect on at least one other person. I often look around and notice how miserable people look, with frowns on their faces. I call it the "smelling onions" look. They say it might be easier to smile than to frown. Smile as often as possible.

August 16

Affirmation: Today I will stop fighting with my past.

When you look back, do so lovingly. When you think about the future, do so with joyful anticipation. The past is gone; the future is yet to be seen. All we have is now. Try not to waste it. Being in the moment is not easy for those who live in the past. Do you often find yourself in misery because you won't let go of the past and you ruminate over what could or should have been?

It can be difficult, or seemingly impossible, to let go of the pain when you feel you have been hurt or wronged in some way. Building new, healthier thoughts, feelings, and attitudes is the only way to change how you feel. Change how you think, and you change how you feel. What you need to do when you find yourself harboring resentment is to change the way you look at things!

Are you, or is someone you know, unwilling or unable to let go of negative feelings, hurt or injustice, or the guilt and shame of the past? You cease to give power to that which haunts you when you do the repair work wholeheartedly and begin to turn a bad situation around. When thoughts of the past creep into your awareness, counter what you would normally think with different, more loving thoughts of what is good in your life at this moment. Then you can move past your past.

August 17

Affirmation: Today I will show love, offer hope, and spread joy.

Happiness multiplies or easily diminishes. Happiness is inherent within us as spiritual beings. It's part of who we are and how we are created. It exists between our breaths. It is right there between our thoughts. Happiness is not to be hoarded, held onto tightly, or, for that matter, held onto at all. Happiness is intensified when offered to, shared with, and given to others. What you give you receive. In order to be loved, show love. In order to experience hope, offer hope. If you want to feel joy, spread joy whenever possible. Love, hope, and joy complement each other. The feelings are interrelated.

August 18

Affirmation: Today I will find a way to make it work.

Great relationships are not great because there isn't any conflict. Relationships are great when those involved work hard and care enough to find a way to make it work. When you want to walk away, turn around. Why? Because unless you work out what it is that you can do better, you will take those faults with you into your next relationship. When trouble comes, let go of your anger. Let go of your fear. Take responsibility for your wrongdoing, and stop hurting yourself and your partner. Be kind, loving, and gentle with yourself and others. Ask for help. Listen to others who love you. Do not blame others for your mistakes. Stay if you can, and leave if you must.

August 19

Affirmation: I am letting go of what I am so angry about and whom I am so angry with.

Perhaps you hold grudges. Maybe hanging onto resentment is second nature for you. You weren't meant to be this way. You are programmed to be happy and at peace. Why then is harboring resentment, fear, and hatred so prevalent? Why do we find fault with our friends and loved ones? Is being angry all the time really who you are?

The key to letting go and moving on is recognizing that others in your life do not have to agree with you or think as you do. We have unfounded expectations of those we are with. When people don't act a certain way, we get angry and frustrated and begin backing away by saying terrible things and getting stressed out, angry, and hurt. Letting go of friendships and moving on can be a very good thing. Perhaps the other person wants to let go of the relationship also. You never know. The best way I know how to stop being angry at a loved one is to send that person love. Whenever I feel like being angry, I change my thoughts and send him or her feelings of connectedness even though we are no longer together. Happiness happens; I am more relaxed and content.

August 20

Affirmation: Today I will leave my comfort zone and be still.

I can really clear my head when I take a walk. Sometimes I go to the park. Sometimes I go for a ride in my car and pull into a place that is quiet, and I simply look at the sky. Why? Because that is when the problems of the world go away, my spirit is open to clarity, and my heart is open to suggestion. Beautiful surroundings bring forth the inner beauty and the inner good thoughts that have been repressed or forgotten because of all the stress in the world that tunes it out. When we are children we play in the sun and the sand all day. We are innocent. As adults we must get in touch with that purity to make sound decisions and to take moments just to breathe. That's an escape, yes, but more time away is needed than we actually take. Some people meditate daily. This is simply the truest form of obtaining clarity.

August 21

Affirmation: Today I will be friendly.
I will open my heart to others.

When you are alone, sometimes all you need is for someone to say hello or give you a hand. Perhaps a smile or a kind word is all it takes to feel appreciated. Why then is it so difficult to offer a smile to a stranger or to help someone out? Is it because you are afraid that you might be harmed or that by helping you are enabling that person in some way? Hopefully you know when to give and when to refrain. It's a gut instinct to know who and when to trust. When you don't go with your gut instinct, you might regret or at the very least think better about your choices. Reach out to others, and have faith in your decision. Reach out to others in a loving, giving and safe way. When an opportunity presents itself, be there for someone in need.

August 22

Affirmation: Today I will remember the power of love in my life.

It might not be an everyday sighting, but when you witness two people holding hands, you know that love is not just for the young. The moms and dads on the subway holding their children on their laps, the parents dropping their child off to college, or the aunts, uncles, and cousins playing together on the beach are all a spectacle for the gods. Love can be seen in the hundreds of thousands of situations when men or women hold the hands of their loved ones in their declining years. Love without fear. Being in public with your beloved without persecution, shame, or fear is a blessing, a human right and, once more, a spectacle for the gods.

August 23

Affirmation: I know what is worth keeping in my life.

Success is allowing yourself to make mistakes. You put your heart and soul into your work, and the results are never perfect, but what is produced is an expression of your thoughts and emotions. You've no doubt experienced success and failure in life. From each and every endeavor in your life, you hopefully take away a lesson of what to do and what not to do next time. You must decide what is worth keeping and what to let go of.

When you are creating or working on a project, you must decide how much is too much. When you opt to keep going, you take the risk of losing focus. You run the risk of not being able to recapture the original concept and design. Editing and revising are key. So it is in life.

When there is an opportunity to scale down, consider it. However, always be aware of who and what matters in your life. Treasure and value the people, places, and things that are good to you and good for you. We all are diverse and complex. Take what is worth keeping, and gently let the rest go.

August 24

Affirmation: I will not judge or hold back my love today.

In our home the rule is that if you are angry with someone and have said or done something to hurt that person in any way, you don't have to say you are sorry; you just simply say, "Let's turn this around." This is not apologizing, per se, because in the moment of a heated exchange you or the other person(s) might not be ready to say *I'm sorry*. What you can do is offer to turn it around by stopping the fighting, taking a moment, and then either walking away and coming back with the resolve not to go there again or stopping and cutting it out until you are ready to work it out. In other words, the people we love are so necessary to our lives that it is hurtful and painful to stay angry at each other.

August 25

Affirmation: I got this.

You can do it. The power is within you. Whatever task you are contemplating can be done with determination, confidence, and courage. No one says it will be easy. But we all have the capacity to begin, stick with it, and complete whatever it is we set out to do.

Too often people look to outside sources for approval and validation, asking questions like "What should I do?" "What would you do?" or "Should I do something different?" or "What do you think?"

When you were young you looked to your parents and teachers for direction and answers to your questions. Time passed and perhaps you looked to friends and continued to rely on the adults in your life. There comes a point in everyone's life when you must think for yourself and make up your own mind. If at a crossroad and paralyzed with the gravity of making up your mind and choosing what it is that you want in life, it is good to seek guidance. Rely on others you love and trust, but ultimately know that the final decision is yours.

August 26

Affirmation: Today I will give it my all, and tomorrow I will do the same.

Persistence is the key to being the best at whatever it is that we set our minds to. If you begin something and hate it, move on. But if you attempt something new—even if you don't have all the talent and knowledge required yet it sparks joy and happiness—then by all means continue. Don't let your inner critic hold you back.

If you are amazed at how much you enjoy playing an instrument or picking up a paintbrush, then by all means continue. No matter how "off in the distance" your first solo attempt may appear, it is a start. "A race of a million miles begins with one step."

What is it that you have always thought of doing but have yet to give it a shot? Think about it. Visualize your dream, your passion, and your desire. Prepare and then go for it. If you venture nowhere, nothing is realized. I wish you fun along the way.

August 27

Affirmation: Today I will connect to my source of love and strength through prayer.

Prayer is simply talking to God. Prayer is a longing of the soul. It is not just asking; it is contemplating and meditating on what you desire. Your God is what gives you strength, courage, and the will to be the best person you can be. It is the source that allows you to eliminate negativity and alleviate pain in your life. Prayer is connecting with the source of strength and love.

Prayer has the power to free you from being in control of all things at all times. Prayer transcends thoughts and actions. It is a connection with an energy that brings forth light and goodness. Prayer is not talking to evil. It does not connect with hatred or fuel animosity.

We pray for guidance, forgiveness, direction, or expression of our thoughts and emotions. Thus, people pray for many reasons, such as personal growth or for the sake of others. If you see prayer as useless, have gotten away from a prayer life, or haven't yet experienced the power of prayer, now is a good time to consider giving prayer and meditation a chance. Prayer is simply being still and waiting for the answers. It is a belief that peace, love, and grace will come to you in body, mind, and spirit if you sincerely connect with your source with an openness to receive.

August 28

Affirmation: Today I will be me without any pretense.

Be yourself. You've heard it a million times. What exactly does that mean? When you were a child, chances are that parents, teachers, and even strangers corrected you and told you to act differently or better. Chances are you were scolded for saying something funny or acting silly. Whenever you were being authentic, it was taken as being inappropriate, at the wrong place or the wrong time. The message continued to be "You're wrong."

Today's generation continues to be scrutinized for their behavior; hopefully they are also praised for spreading their wings, showcasing their talents, and not being afraid to be creative and playful.

You are truly being yourself when you like who you are. When you like yourself, you are unlike anyone else. If others find that difficult, it doesn't matter. What matters is that you are being yourself and you like who you are. When you are a loving version of yourself, you will soon find that you are creating your own style.

August 29

Affirmation: I ask for help when needed.

If help is offered in the right way, people rarely turn it down. Yet when help is offered and the recipient does not want or need help, that can be a problem. Some people refuse help because in the past, help came with a price; it was not offered lovingly, or it was offered with strings attached.

What do you do when you need help? Help could be in the form of a very small gesture or assisting someone in a dire situation. Some people do not ask for help in any circumstance. When you need help, do you refuse to ask or refuse to accept it? Do you know who to go to when you are in need? Do you have people in your life that you trust? You might think these are basic questions not even worth talking about, but the fact is that many people find it extremely difficult and, therefore, do not ask for help under any circumstances. Asking for help depends on the person and the situation. Asking for help depends on hundreds of factors. It is important to know not only who to go to but that help, in fact, is needed. You might be in denial of any problem at all.

August 30

Affirmation: Today I will let go of a grudge I have been hanging onto for way too long.

A grudge is not letting go of persistent, unresolved issues or resentment resulting from a past insult or injury. Holding a grudge is being resentfully unwilling to give, grant, or allow peace and understanding in a situation. Grudges start when we blame someone else for when we feel hurt or misunderstood. When we feel wronged, perhaps we hold it against the other person rather than talking it out and coming to an agreed-upon resolution or conclusion.

To move past a grudge and let it go completely, you must first take responsibility for your actions. Reconcile with the person or persons against whom you are holding a grudge. You must let go of the pain and heartache; let go of the feelings of anger, resentment, and injustice.

When someone does something wrong to you, what that person did is not your fault, but how you react is. What another person does to you is not because of you; it is because of a flaw or resentment he or she harbors. Stop feeling personally offended, and recognize it is about that person, not you. Move on past it. The only thing holding a grudge does is make us angry, resentful, and hate filled. Not only does the relationship with the person we are unable to forgive suffer, but our relationships with other loved ones suffer because of the unresolved anger. We all suffer times in our lives when we are hurt and wounded by what others have said or did. You don't have to be in that person's life anymore. You certainly can walk away. But walk away and choose to forgive. Remember—nothing you say or do has the power to make another person be mean or hurtful to you. It's the other person's problem, not yours.

August 31

Affirmation: The future is mine to behold.

What you focus on expands. The future is coming—that's for certain. You can foresee what your future will look like by knowing you are the captain of your ship. You create the future as much as you created your past. Create, design, and map out your journey. The future is a blank canvas.

The power is yours to shape the future. The key is not to worry and not to be afraid of the future. Be smart, and think about what it is that you need, want, and desire. When you follow the path, you just might be amazed to experience things *are* going your way—not at first perhaps, but by setting concrete goals and objectives and following your destiny, before long you might just find you are where you want to be. You are where you are meant to be.

September

International Self-Awareness Month

September 1

Affirmation: Help will come when I sincerely ask for it.

How many times have you felt as if you were at your wit's end? Maybe you're at that point now. When you're sad, anxious, or overwhelmed, take a moment to regroup, collect your thoughts, and give yourself time to pray or meditate. Take a long, slow breath, and wait for an answer. An answer will show up.

I hope those moments are distant memories and you are in a healthy time in your life, emotionally, mentally, and physically. If you are in that good place, take a moment to look back on those low times in your life. When you were at your lowest point, did something or someone come along to help you through? Keep those good thoughts with you as a reminder that you have within you the strength, resilience, and ability to persevere in times of trouble.

September 2

Affirmation: Today I will make room for change in my life.

I have met and worked with so many people who profess they hate change. When I think of those individuals, I think of a grumpy old man set in his ways, unwilling to yield to the changing times. Yet change is difficult, if not frightening, to a lot of people.

You feel safe in certain situations yet become uncomfortable at other times because you feel awkward or less than. Many people shy away from situations or advancements, because they fear the unknown. They fear what might happen.

Some people cannot abide things being out of order or not being in control; this may be a form of obsessive-compulsive disorder, which requires mental health professional intervention. Aside from these extremes, we all have a degree of angst when we find ourselves outside of our comfort zones. Taking chances and calculated risks is what we are called to do hundreds of times a day. Risk taking can come in many ways, shapes, and forms, but to shut down and not try new things is not allowing the natural progression to work in your life. Rather, you may stay stuck. Change may be anxiety producing for some, but to acknowledge that change is going to come is the healthy choice for all of us. Staying with what makes you happy can be a very good thing, but when it isn't working anymore, it's time to change.

Make choices, try new options and avenues, and keep the door open to a brighter tomorrow. Change is going to happen every minute of every day. Accept change.

September 3

Affirmation: Today I will trust my gut instinct.

Trust yourself. It sounds simple, yet for many of us, trusting our instincts is one of the hardest concepts to live by. Trust your instincts. It sounds like basic advice, right? Take a minute or two to think of a time when you had a major life decision and you knew what was best in that situation. Now think back to how often you doubted yourself, worried, and agonized over that decision. You asked everyone you knew and loved (and even those you didn't) for their input, just to go with what you thought was right; or, if you didn't go with your gut, you found that you made the wrong choice for you.

On the other hand, what happened in those circumstances when you didn't go with your own instinct and went with what others thought was best for you? Did it work out? Trusting in yourself is difficult when that voice inside of you tells you that you are somehow not equipped to make sound choices. It is that feeling of inadequacy that prevents you from being the best you can be. You pass up opportunities and let go of jobs, schooling, or relationships because you are reluctant to change, for fear of failure or succeeding. Go with your gut, and you will make the right choice. It might not be a perfect solution, but it will be what you know is best.

September 4

Affirmation: I choose to understand others and myself better.

Understanding others is vital to establishing and maintaining healthy relationships, yet many have no idea what other people are going through or have gone through in their lives. We may take for granted that everything must be all right with them and their circumstances; otherwise they would have said something. I know from personal experience that I rarely let people know when I am hurting. I wait to call on friends until I am doing well and retreat into myself when I am not in a good place. I'm certain this is the way with many others.

Granted, we can't know if someone is hurting unless that person tells us, but we can be kind so that we are not adding to his or her troubles. In other words, we do no harm.

When we understand other people and other cultures, we have insight into their customs and behaviors. What people want is to be heard and understood. It's a universal principle that people want to be happy and don't want to suffer. Many wars could be averted if people learned to accept one another and better understand the differences that separate us along with the commonalities that connect us. Peace can only exist when everyone is in a place of contentment, a place where they are satisfied, a place where their voices are heard. It's not quantum physics.

September 5

Affirmation: Today I will help another person. I will help myself.

It feels just as good to help others as it does for others to be there for you. When you give of yourself, there is a degree of risk. Some people think that helping others in their time of need may be inviting trouble. I have lived my life cautiously yet open to the possibility that helping others, particularly strangers, is what I am called to do.

At some point in our lives, we all have been called on to help someone else out. When you witness someone who is hurt, do you stop and help or keep on going, assuming that someone else will come along? How many times have we all walked by a person on the street down on his or her luck? We are called upon to help others.

I am not here to judge what anyone else does or doesn't do. You know when you could be helping out more than you're doing now. The signs are all around you. The need is all around you. In the split second that you hesitate when you see someone in need, take a moment and reconsider walking by and doing something, anything, to make that person's plight a little easier. Say a simple prayer or blessing on that person. What you might think is insignificant may be huge to someone in need.

September 6

Affirmation: When we learn to let go of negativity, we can cherish the memories of all that was good.

Anger, hurt, and resentment are emotions generally saved for those to whom you are closest. When you feel hurt, slighted, or even abused, your natural tendency seems to be getting angry and lashing out. Or perhaps you misdirect your negativity to someone who has nothing to do with your pain and is innocent and undeserving of your wrath. Or maybe you are the type of person who says nothing and bottles up negative emotions until the hurt and pain do internal or external damage. Perhaps you self-medicate the pain and anxiety with sex, drugs, overeating, or self-abuse in some form, which leads to failed relationships, low self-esteem, illness, or a damaged self-awareness and self-image.

All this is overwhelming and damaging. A new and fresh perspective is warranted. A more enlightened sense of self, others, and the world in general can be frightening. However, letting go of your fears, negative thinking, addiction, or any kind of self-loathing behavior will set you free, and you just might see the world in a more positive, loving way.

September 7

Affirmation: Today I will focus on what matters. I will keep it simple.

I was not a business major and never thought that someday I would own my own business. But I do now, and I live by "less is best." I have learned that the more work I generate for myself, the more I am responsible for. Simplify. Do good, quality work; anything else is not needed. When you find yourself overworked, step back and take a look at the quality of life at the moment. Are you where you want to be? Are you doing what you want to be doing? Are you doing and saying things that are authentically you?

So many people do not take breaks at work, at school, or even at home. They eat lunch at their desks or skip meals altogether. Even worse, they have pizza and fast food five days a week. A lot of folks do not exercise or take care of their health, because they say they are "too busy." Seriously? This is one of the most ridiculous excuses for being overstressed, overweight, and overwrought. You are too busy doing what? Bosses, teachers, and employees must take a stand and insist on periodic breaks throughout the day. Prevent burnout. Let's do lunch!

September 8

Affirmation: I am proud of myself.

Be yourself, love the person you are, and be proud. You make choices every minute of every day. When you make well-thought- out choices, you can be proud. When you live your life authentically, you can be proud. When you have a dream and continue on in the direction of your goals, you can be proud. When you do the right thing and live your life as best as you can, no matter how difficult your circumstances are, you can be proud.

What does it mean to have sound principles and pride in yourself, your work, and your relationships amidst change and chaos? It means that when your life is going forward, there are standards that you won't compromise. There are things you aren't willing to do to get ahead; ethical decisions hold you firm to the positive way in which you choose to live your life. You want to be fair and honest and help others along the way. This is living your life in a way that you can be proud of.

September 9

Affirmation: Today I will recognize the power of light in my life.

Light is your friend. It is also an antidote. Open the shade on a sunny day, and let the light in. Light has restorative properties. Let your light shine. When you are like the lighthouse and your inner light is turned off, you attract nothing and no one. This is a basic concept. However, shining your inner light is what you are called to do. Become a beacon of light to others. There are times when you are called to be the light in the darkness. Now is that time. Do not fear the darkness; shine your light!

September 10

Affirmation: I will let go of the need to reward myself with more stuff.

If the price is too high, you can't afford it. Why is it that we convince ourselves that we deserve certain things? Look around you. How many friends, family members, and neighbors (perhaps even you) are overextended? Why is it that we convince ourselves that we deserve certain things when it is not in our best interest to have them? External gratification is false gratification. The reality is that if you are not content on the inside, nothing that you can buy is going to make you feel better overall.

Don't give in to retail therapy! Overspending might seem like a temporary fix, but so are drugs and alcohol. Is it worth the cost in the long run when you are living paycheck to paycheck?

Our elders lived within their means before MasterCard and Visa came along. Baby boomers are the first generation to buy with plastic. Granted, there is a time and place for putting off payment until later, but only when later comes and you have the cold, hard cash to make the payment.

So many people are in debt. What that means is many are staying awake at night trying to figure out a way to pay the bills. It means being continually stressed out, in a constant state of worrying, hiding the bills that come in each month. Why not turn this entitled thinking around and begin to be okay with less?

That sounds easy, right? I am in the throes of cutting back on my discretionary spending, and I find myself angry at times when I don't have what I want when I want it. While at times I spend too much. I try to remember there are others who do not even have enough to eat. Put money away for a rainy day. Give to those less fortunate. Donate to causes and nonprofits that are making a difference. A $500 handbag can put food on the table for an entire village.

September 11

Affirmation: Today will be a day of reflection. I will honor my time with loved ones. We will never forget 9/11/01.

Every year on September 11, I feel sad. I listen to the names on the roll call at Ground Zero on the morning news shows. I listen for my friends' names and the names of loved ones who perished in the most horrific atrocity our nation has yet to face in our lifetime. September 11 changed our country, and it changed the people of our nation. I remember the mourners of the heroes who perished in the towers and the first responders who lost their lives saving others. The days to follow were a blur. The country mourned. Today we set aside this day to once again mourn the tragedy of that beautiful, blue-skied September morning. In New York City; Washington, DC; and the fields of Stonycreek Township, Pennsylvania, we were there. We hurt. We cry. Never be ashamed to cry.

We must grieve. A grieving heart will heal in time, and when it does, the memory of your beloved will be etched inside to comfort you, and the sky will be blue again.

September 12

Affirmation: Today I will break free from unhappiness.

No one wants to be unhappy. Everyone wants to be happy. Why then is happiness so elusive for so many? How come you can't be happy all the time? People say life would be boring if everyone was always happy. I certainly would like to give forever happy a try. The alternative is being unhappy with your situation, your life, and yourself. We all want just that little bit more. If you were just a little prettier or a little smarter or richer, you'd be happier. It is the elusive butterfly. The more you chase happiness, the more difficult it is to catch, but when you sit still and are patient, it shows up.

Perhaps you are so entrenched in being unhappy that when happiness shows up, you blink and it's gone. You may miss the subtle signs and momentary glimpses of joy and not even know it. Happiness is not a constant feeling. It comes in moments—watching a flower bloom or giving a smile away. You get hundreds of moments throughout the day to be happy that might last if uninterrupted. That's basically it. Happiness is a state of contentment and well-being. It's being balanced in body, mind, and spirit. It is pleasurable and satisfying.

Happiness is being at peace and feeling satisfied. With that definition we can strive to be satisfied in every part of life. Being satisfied is when your needs and wants are being met, and you feel heard and understood. Today, begin to look at life in terms of being grateful and satisfied. Happiness will show up.

September 13

Affirmation: Today I will stop chasing the poisonous snake that bit me.

Some people think they don't deserve a better life. They continue on broken paths, ones that do not make them happy.

They continue on, knowing that this is not the life they chose. They stay with those who hurt them. They fear they can't change, but the fact is we all can. We can turn it around. We can change our course.

Pain exists. Without pain there is no joy. When the snake comes your way, get help or take action, but do not chase the danger. You very well might get harmed. You will feel the pain. Take inventory of the negativity and poisons in your life. Joy, happiness, and help from others will be found when you stop chasing the bad things in life. You need to get out of your own way.

September 14

Affirmation: Today I will not listen to the cynic in my head. I will keep my head in the clouds, if only for the moment.

Think clearly and consciously, but don't ever let someone convince you to get your head out of the clouds. That is where art and beauty exist. Daydreaming, fantasizing, wishing, and hoping are all very meaningful and powerful tools we have at our disposal. Letting our thoughts travel is not always a bad thing. Is there a time and place for dreaming, or is any time a good time to go inside your fantasy world? What we truly want is in those hopes, dreams, and desires. So it must not be a bad place to be.

Do not postpone dreaming. Do not postpone joy. Without daydreaming on a subway or fantasizing in line at the supermarket, even wishing on a star, the life we have might have taken a different path.

September 15

Affirmation: Today I will wait for healing to happen.

Without a doubt, getting outside, walking to a park, or sitting alone on a beach is the ultimate cure for much or all of our bad moments in life. Yet when faced with sadness or rejection, the last thing we find ourselves doing is the very thing that will help the most. Changing scenery or doing something out of the ordinary does the spirit good. (It also does the body good!) Getting away from your desk, out of your room, or out of the empty apartment, or choosing to be in the woods, on a path, or by a lake brings renewal, a sense that there is some force outside yourself in charge and that you can let go of your troubles, if only for an hour, to enjoy the beauty and the wonder of nature.

Time heals all wounds. When the world seems to be falling apart around you, take a moment to go for a walk. Don't react in the moment. The moment will pass, and the situation will improve with patience. The immediacy of any trial will diminish given time. Take a moment to divert yourself, and when you return to the problem at hand, you will be able to look at your sorrow and disappointment with a new and brighter perspective. Nothing erases the pain, but time will make it somehow easier to bear.

Patience is a great healer. Patience is the ability to trust, knowing everything will work out. Patience is letting go of control and waiting for the time to be right. If you walk away and take a few minutes to regroup, you very well may come back with a different perspective. Nature, time, and patience are my health and wellness model.

September 16

Affirmation: We are here to love each other, not just when it is convenient.

When you are having a bad day and find it difficult to make it through, perhaps the last thing you want to do is be nice. You may want everyone to notice that you are feeling bad and wait for the phone to ring or a loved one to notice and comfort you in some way, shape, or form. You may assume that person will cheer you up, because you need cheering up.

What makes a lousy mood better is when you reach out to others. If you're in a rut or annoyed, do something nice for someone, like giving a smile away. When you *act as if* and do something nice for someone else, you can improve your mood dramatically.

If you turn the tide and take the children to the park, you will benefit the most. You can turn the tide by preparing a meal and calling a friend to join you. If you are in a position where you are new at work or have just moved into a new apartment and don't have loved ones around, go to a meeting at the library or local house of worship. Get involved with people who might need what you have to offer. Volunteering or offering kindness to others creates true win-win scenarios.

September 17

Affirmation: My reality is my truth.

Your reality and your perception are your truth. So many times you find you are second-guessing yourself. *Am I right? Did I make the right decision?* The answer is always a resounding yes. Do your best, and be impeccable with what you say. If, at any time, you are not authentic or honest with yourself or others, you are doing yourself a disservice.

Many people subscribe to the theory that their reality isn't always the best or maybe they're not right. Many people think that they know best. No one is right all the time. What is right for you might not be right for someone else. You can't determine if someone is wrong or right, because you can never be certain.

Don't speak words that you will have to cover up. Your words are your most important tool by which to live your life authentically and out loud. What you know for certain is real. Your intentions are the basis of your truth.

September 18

Affirmation: Today I will seek out silence.

Silence is a very scary proposition for many people. We turn on the television or radio, play the iPod, call a friend, or do anything to fill the void with noise. If there is no sound, we are left with our thoughts. For many, this is a very uncomfortable position.

Personally, I like quiet. I like the quiet of the forest, the quiet of the beach, and a quiet church. I don't like to have noise just to fill the space in between activities, chores, thoughts, feelings, or desires.

It is in the quiet that our questions are answered. It is in the quiet times that we can reflect. When it is quiet, we can take a moment to breathe. Why then is silence so foreign to some? Distraction, distraction, distraction! With the high-tech existence in which we now find ourselves, solitude or the absence of noise is unsettling, uncomfortable, and perhaps even frightening. It feels lonely. It makes us get in touch with the self that we may be trying to avoid. Sound then can be considered an addiction, like any other way of coping. It's not always healthy to have noise in the background at all times, but if there is no silence, we will forget the art of listening.

September 19

Affirmation: When I find myself worried, anxious, or scared, I will take a moment to breathe.

Breathing is the ultimate source of life, it is the source of (S)pirit in our lives. When you cease breathing, you die. When you are not focused on your breathing, you are unaware of the spirit within you. Just breathe. Telling someone to breathe is becoming trendy, yet it is highly effective. Instead of cursing, yelling, or screaming at someone who is offending you with words or actions, help that person to become aware that he or she needs to calm down. We can model this by simply taking a breath and calming ourselves down.

Throughout our busy days and hurried lives it is easy to become upset, overwrought, and angry. Anger is normal. It is how you deal with your anger that becomes an issue. Are you passive or aggressive, or are you able to be assertive? Being assertive means getting your needs and wants met without hurting anybody else. People who are assertive take the time to pause and think about how they respond and how they act.

When you are worried or anxious, do you think of the worst-case scenario? Are you convinced that trouble is around the corner, and you fear doom and gloom? Are you scared that the sky is falling? Take a moment out of the trouble that surrounds you, and then pause to reflect, consider the possibilities, and breathe. You will find that your worry will abate.

September 20

Affirmation: I need help.

Three little words, when said at the right time in the right place, can be life altering. Can you do everything on your own? Of course not, silly! From the earliest stages of life, you have needed assistance with just about everything until you obtained mastery. Still, every now and then, you need someone else's expertise or assistance. Why then is it so difficult for people to ask for help? The ego is so strong and exerts so much control that some folks find it difficult, if not impossible, to admit they need help.

When you find yourself in need of assistance with anything in your life, look to where you need to be. Seek out people whom you can trust. A believer or nonbeliever asks for guidance, and the spiritual path he or she seeks presents itself. Assistance is there for the asking.

How wonderful does it feel when someone asks you for help? You're glad to do so, and it makes you feel better to know you can help out, if only in a small way. By not asking for help, you are not only denying yourself a better situation in life, but you are also denying your loved ones, friends, and community to become better people. You are denying them the chance to put their knowledge, ability, and talents to work for the benefits of others.

Not asking for help comes from a place of stubbornness, pride, and low self-esteem. People who don't ask for help think they are able to do things by themselves without help from anyone.

When you find yourself in need of assistance with any task, large or small, seek out people you can trust to get you where you need to be. Some people are afraid they will become too reliant on others. Here is a perfect opportunity to practice balance in your life. Independent, dependent, interdependent—which will it be?

September 21

Affirmation: Today I will let go of control; it doesn't work.

Control is not always a good thing. People say, "I am out of control," as if it was a negative thing. "Control yourself," we are told when we are acting out, crying, or showing anger. To some degree being in control is better than being out of control; that is indisputable. The control I am referring to is when someone needs to be in control at all times, in all situations, with everyone in his or her life. There is a time and place for having full charge of the situation. Overly controlling people operate from two very negative spaces. They suffer from fear and lack of faith. Actually, fear is the lack of faith. Lately I have been putting this theory to the test. I walk away from a situation when my family is making plans. I leave the room when a discussion is happening that I really am not involved with. I have begun to wait until someone asks for my input, and I am finding that I am avoiding a lot of unnecessary confrontations. When we let go, we find that the people in our lives are less combative than before.

When parents have young children, they feel the need to know what is best. This need spills over into their children's adolescence and teenage years and also has the potential to infiltrate their relationships with their spouses. I see young adults all the time who tell me they do not feel heard or understood. Parents feel they need to control their children so they don't do drugs, get bad grades, or fall into the wrong crowd. Actually, overprotective control can lead children to act out and rebel. The best way to pull back when the need to control strikes is to take a step back, recognize that other people may have better ideas, and know there are times when control is not a good thing. Recognize what you are afraid of, and let your faith in others and your faith in God take over.

September 22

Affirmation: Today I will speak up.

Whether or not you are comfortable speaking is entirely personal. Everyone feels differently about talking. Some talk constantly. This comes from fear and anxiety. What is lacking in quality is made up in quantity. Some people hardly say anything—again, possibly out of fear. They're afraid of saying the wrong thing. It certainly is a dilemma for most people. For some, communicating can be a real problem.

Research shows speaking in public is one of the greatest fears in life. It can feel like an out-of-body experience. For some, well, it's just never going to happen. Speaking and communicating are certainly art forms.

If you are knowledgeable and comfortable with yourself, it's much easier to go through life knowing your words will come out exactly the way you intended.

Be careful to watch your tongue when you are mad, hurt, or upset. This is probably the best time to keep quiet. Balance your words, and temper your tongue.

September 23

Affirmation: Today I will determine where I want to be.

Determination is the act of resolving a question by reason or argument. It's the act of deciding definitely and firmly. Knowing what you want, who you are, what is important to you, and whom you want to be with in your life are all determined by you and you alone. Being uncertain or ill at ease with your wants and desires is being in a state of confusion and apathy. When you make decisions for yourself and your future, you get there by sheer determination; you make a conscious effort to set a path and do what it takes to get to your goals. When you feel confident and determined that you are in a healthy, balanced place in your life, you create contentment, inner peace, and happiness for yourself and those around you.

September 24

Affirmation: Today I will try to stay on the path of goodness.

First and foremost, ask yourself why, what, where, and for whom. What are you doing in your life, and for whom? Where is the road taking you, and why? Things will go wrong. Things don't always go according to plan. Things turn out differently from what you hoped would happen or what you counted on to take place. No one lives a charmed life where everything turns out the way it should. Contrary to popular thinking, the Joneses don't always have it better than you do.

Never go along with a situation that isn't in your best interest. You always have a choice. Don't give up or give in. It's easy to turn a situation into a catastrophe and convince yourself that what happened or what might happen is so bad that you won't be able to handle it.

How can you think differently and steer away from those faulty, unskilled thoughts that lead to unpleasant and uncomfortable feelings? How can you look at the situation differently? What is a different approach you can cultivate? What is a different interpretation that you can offer yourself to deal effectively with the difficulty without succumbing to it? Think about how you can de-catastrophize, de-emphasize, and demolish the temptation to go along with the things that will go wrong. Change direction, and get back on the path to goodness. Make a conscious effort to go along with right-minded people, not always like-minded people in your life, who are headed in a positive direction.

September 25

Affirmation: Today I will walk in humility, knowing that I am the best version of myself.

Fame and recognition are collectively ego based. If you want to be the center of attention, go for it, but that might not be the easiest way or the most satisfying way to go. If you are driven by being the best and the brightest, making the most money, and having the most expensive things, it is very possible and highly probable that you will not always find that your accomplishments are truly deserved or even warranted. Recognition, achievement, and accomplishment are respected goals if you are working toward a higher good and are fair and honest along the way.

The lesson is to want what you have and have what you want. Be okay with what you have accomplished and what your future may hold for you. If you never have fame and fortune, you might think you're missing out or feel deprived or even jealous. You might make excuses for you meager life. However, the reality is that you must first attain your goals to know that being happy with where you are in the moment is all that really matters.

What is the answer? It is love, kindness, faith, healthy relationships, understanding, and caring, as well as the knowledge that you are a child of the universe—no better and no worse than anyone else. Be humble. Be yourself.

September 26

Affirmation: Today I will seek to find my bliss.

Are you becoming aware of the importance of being present in the moment and what it's like to no longer live in the past or worry about the future? When you experience being still and without worry, you begin to feel calm, relaxed, and rejuvenated. It is blissful. It's like a day at the spa!

Real consequences to living in the past and worrying about the future include the potential for high blood pressure, digestive ailments, migraines, stroke, and a multitude of other physical ailments. Not being present in body, mind, and spirit can lead to failed relationships and missed opportunities. Being in the moment and practicing the awareness of your breathing are accomplished through meditation, prayer or chanting. Being alone, listening to soft music and the rhythms of nature, and being in a quiet place lead to self-actualization and joy.

September 27

Affirmation: I am satisfied. In this moment I am happy with what I have.

Do you know someone (or are you that someone) who is waiting for something, anything, to happen or come along to make them happy? "If I just ______________________________ or get a ______________________________, or if someone else ______________________________ I will be happy." Who hasn't felt this way at one time or another? The truth is that nothing—"no thing"—will ultimately make us happy. Getting the thing we want is only a temporary feel-good moment. If we are accustomed to associating our happiness with the acquisition of things, then it is just a matter of time before we get what we want, become happy, and then turn toward wanting something else. Accumulating money or material things doesn't have to do with happiness. Rich people can be miserable, and those with seemingly less can be as happy as can be. What's the common denominator other than what you have or don't have? It's what you think about your life. Are you positive about your life? Do you celebrate your family, your lot in life? Do you celebrate who you are and how far you have come? To be really happy, focus on and identify ways of recognizing that you can enjoy the abundance of your present circumstances. Be satisfied. Right this moment, be happy with what you have.

September 28

Affirmation: I know what is worth keeping in my life.

I have always loved art, music, dance, and literature. I suppose I operate on the right side of my brain. As it turns out I have never been a proponent of left-brain/right-brain or type A/type B personality typecasting. The theories are groundbreaking and fascinating. Scientific research has championed great insight into brain function and has enhanced the advancements in the behavioral sciences. However, I believe we all are more diverse and complex than being one or the other.

If you are stuck in a rut, stuck in a cubicle, and never get out to sing and dance, why not? If you want to learn something completely different from what you are used to, give it a try.

Music educators have told me that the most important reason for keeping music programs in our public schools is that learning an instrument exercises a part of the brain that is not commonly exercised. The goal of advancing the arts is to develop competency and personal development.

I suggest we get out of our boxes, try something different, and make as many mistakes as we want to. You cannot play the violin unless you are painfully inept at it first (unless you are a prodigy, which I certainly am not).

I have made many embarrassing mistakes that I wish no one had witnessed; however, I did venture out and take lessons in whatever it was that I was called to do. When you opt to keep going, you take the risk of failure. Creativity is when you make mistakes. Art is when you have the insight to know which pieces to keep.

September 29

Affirmation: Normal is a line on which nobody walks.

Who, at some point in his or her life, hasn't felt crazy, confused, minimalized, out of the loop, or destructive? Hopefully for you it wasn't traumatic or devastating and you got through relatively unscathed. In life, when you are overwhelmed, you are the most vulnerable. You are vulnerable to self-criticism and self-doubt. Life feels like it is steering out of control.

This is a good time to take a "mental health day." Relax. Don't do anything stressful or anything that requires you to be on your game. Why? Perhaps you aren't balanced out right now. Heal. Stress-induced illness is illness just the same. Take care of yourself, and then get back in the game. Get back to your daily routine after you have rested and are rejuvenated.

When you are ready, take time to laugh and see the humor in your situation. Being able to laugh at yourself is a healing remedy. If your body, mind, and spirit are compromised, it is an opportunity to reassess and make changes. Take every opportunity to minimize the gravity and find the common ground in your situation. At this point, it is important to recognize that you are not alone and it is human to need a time-out every now and then. It is good for the soul, as well as your body and mind.

September 30

Affirmation: I believe in moving forward with honesty and integrity.

When you find yourself in a compromising situation, when you know you are in too deep and you wish you were anywhere but where you are, keep going. Stop and look at what you're doing. Walk away, and then return. Change before what you are trying to avoid escalates. You can do this.

When things are getting out of hand, stop what you are doing. Think about the outcome you are trying to achieve. Leaving a situation, regrouping, and coming back is the epitome of class.

How many times have you walked away from a situation and kept going? No way were you going back. What it takes to be a winner is going back, trying again, and bringing closure in the best possible way. Perhaps that means agreeing to disagree. (If you can't go back, move on.) How you leave a situation is how you will be judged. Be true to yourself, and end disagreements, arguments, and discussions on a positive note. Then, and only then, can you move forward.

October

Diversity Awareness Month

October 1

Affirmation: I no longer focus on the meaning of life; it is within me to create.

If we aren't there for our fellow human beings, who are we there for? We can't help ourselves until we learn to help others. When we pass up an opportunity to be of help to others, we are shutting down a piece of our own humanity. Our humanity is simply what makes us human. Therefore, if we are remiss in giving and being of service to others, we are cut off from love, happiness, and selflessness. We all are like an island unto ourselves. We are alone in the part of us that is cut off from the power of giving. When we serve others, we reap the joy of knowing that someone is better off because of our contribution, however large or small.

October 2

Affirmation: Today I will strive to be more compassionate.

Being compassionate means that you put yourself in that person's position and think long and hard about how you would act or react in a similar situation. Perhaps, given the circumstances, you might behave the same way. Perhaps you have acted poorly toward someone in the past. Perhaps you haven't shown your best side in every situation. Chances are you haven't. After all, you are human.

Do you have someone in mind that is on the receiving end of your negativity and perhaps jealousy? Are you aware of what that person must endure in life? We all suffer, and we all have stories. Some people say they don't care why other people do what they do. They do not excuse others easily. These people may be "walled off" and have hardened their hearts. Perhaps they were not given a second chance.

This type of closed-mindedness can lead to anger and resentment. Perhaps people are set in their negative patterns because they find it difficult to change or they don't know where to begin or how to change. Perhaps they have not been shown compassion so they are unwilling or unable to show kindness to others. Whether you are closed off or are being targeted, look past the action and get to the heart of the problem. All will benefit. Compassion, kindness, and understanding toward one another are the ultimate goals.

October 3

Affirmation: Quiet beauty is God.

Take a moment to be still. It's an amazing feeling. All the chatter is gone, and there's no one bothering you. It's a moment of bliss. What's not to love about that? Why is it that so many people never take the time to be still? In the midst of chaos, we often ramp it up instead of slowing it down. One works, while the alternative doesn't.

The voice that guides you is only audible when there is no interference. You know it when you experience it. When there is complete silence, when you are able to quiet your mind and let go of extraneous chatter, when your thoughts are quieted, you can experience the beauty of clarity. It is meditative and restorative.

If you've never meditated before, now is a good time to start. Listen to meditations on tape, go to a class, or simply practice on your own. Once you allow yourself the gift of silence, you will understand the importance of the restorative qualities of simply letting go of the thoughts of the day and the worries on your mind. Let your burdens go. When you practice meditation, you open yourself up to an alternative perspective on life, a quieter, more peaceful way of dealing with things. You quiet the mind and allow peace and contentment in. It's easy to forget that the answers are within each one of us. Let go of the noise in your life, and find the answers within.

Famous athletes, actors, and highly successful executives meditate regularly. You don't have to change dramatically, travel far, or engage anyone else. You have everything you need. Take a deep breath, be still, and listen. Just listen.

October 4

Affirmation: Today I will lead with kindness.

The warmth of the sun is powerful, and so are you. You have the power to make a bad situation better. You have the power to make someone feel loved and appreciated. You have the power to enjoy your life and have happy and healthy relationships. How? By being kind.

Kindness is a virtue. It's helping someone and not expecting anything in return. Kindness is being nice.

If there is a misunderstanding and someone is giving you a hard time, the best way to handle the situation is with kindness. Attacking the person is only going to escalate an already-bad situation. If someone doubts you or you have a problem trusting someone, be kind. Do not jump to conclusions. Getting angry makes matters worse. Always lead with kindness.

October 5

Affirmation: Today I will be aware of opportunities to expand my open mind.

It is important, if you are guilty of having a closed mind, to replace it with an open one. I'm not suggesting replacing a closed mind with a full one, but rather an open one. Are you open to suggestion and situations that are different from what you are accustomed to? Do you listen to another's point of view that might be different from yours? Are you open to seeing things in a new and different light? People who are closed-minded tend to be full of thoughts, opinions, and ideas that are etched in stone and non-negotiable. People whose minds are closed have difficulty seeing the world any way other than theirs. They tend to have fixed and rigid perceptions and beliefs.

On the other hand, those who strive to have a more open-minded approach to life have a desire to learn and, in doing so, realize just how much they don't know. The beauty of knowing that we don't know everything and, in fact, know very little opens us up to learning more and expanding our horizons. We allow ourselves to be open to new thoughts, ideas, and experiences. "Really, I didn't know that. Please enlighten me."

When encountering a person, group, or situation that is different from our own personal beliefs, values, or preferences, it is important to be aware of how to handle the situation. Ask yourself if you are accepting or being standoffish. Do you make an effort to see things in a way that might be culturally, spiritually, or generationally different from yours? Look for opportunities to expand your horizons, as well as your network of friends. Rather than being judgmental or dismissive, focus on being more inquisitive and understanding. Try to realize that there is more going on than you are aware of. Keep that mind open.

October 6

Affirmation: I am good to myself. I eat well, I exercise, and I take time to rest.

A few days of eating right and exercising, one day of wrongful indulgence, and it's game over. We sometimes get off track, and it seems virtually impossible to restart our health and wellness plan. Does this sound familiar to you? Don't give up. Your body wants you to be healthy. Just ask it.

When you eat fatty or sugary foods, your body reacts in a negative way. Your skin, energy level, and waist size are poorly affected. Sometimes you even feel sick. Junk food is just that: junk. It's convenient and tastes good, but in the long run it is bad, pure and simple.

So how do you begin a lifestyle of eating the right foods and cutting out the fats and sweets? The only way you can eat the right food is to have it at home. You can't eat what you don't have in your pantry. This is a problem for people who don't like grocery shopping. You might fear running into people when you are not looking your best, or you might want to be left alone when picking out your produce. If you are overworked and overtired, going to the supermarket can be a nightmare. If you don't mind your daily or weekly shopping trip, go for it. But if you are reluctant and go to the store kicking and screaming, there are tricks to get around the "I hate to grocery shop" blues.

Try going to the grocery store at different times of the day; pick a time when you are feeling positive and productive. Shop online for your groceries. Stores now have websites where you can purchase your items and then pick them up or have them delivered. Or go to the farmer's market on a beautiful day, and have your spirits lifted by the experience of the sights, sounds, and yummy smells. Exchange the unhealthy choices for healthy fruits, meats, and vegetables. What's is in your cart just might make the trip worthwhile.

October 7

Affirmation: Today I will see others' possibilities rather than their flaws.

It is easy to be attracted to people who are seemingly successful and have it all together. That is why they are called the "beautiful people." It is easy because of the assumption that they are not going to hurt you, you don't have to do anything for them, and they are non-threatening. What you think and what you see may be very different. The downtrodden—the kid without shoes or the woman who has difficulty feeding her children—might not be attractive, but they have potential and they have a story. Giving them your attention might be exactly what is needed to have a seed bloom into a beautiful flower that is pleasing to the eye. The eye can be deceiving. Clean yourself up, and look for the beauty in every living creature. It will enhance your inner beauty.

October 8

Affirmation: I am ready for things to turn around for me.

There are good times, and there are bad times. When you're in the dark, and bad things keep happening, it's hard to see the light. There's a chance, however, that with a positive outlook, affirming change can take place quicker than if you continue to weigh yourself down. In other words, if you know that the bad feelings are only temporary and they will pass, you are opening up to the possibility of happier times.

It's all in the vision. It's about the outlook and outcome. Are you stuck, or are you open to positivity? Your emotions are yours to control, and how you control your emotions is with your thoughts. Keep a good thought, be affirming, and stay positive.

October 9

Affirmation: I am at my best when I am helping someone else.

You have strengths that make you unique. What is it that you are blessed with? What are your God-given talents? What do you have that you are able to share with others?

Some people are blessed with creativity, organizational skills, leadership, understanding, a sense of humor, and so on. The list is endless. You have something you can bring to the table. Are you good at asking others for money? Do you have a flair for decorating? Fund-raising, marathons, and charity functions all need volunteers. There is always something that needs to be done, and perhaps you are the person to do it. Teaching your children that they possess skills and talents that can be of use to the larger community in need is invaluable.

Do you have a purpose? Do you do what is necessary to lift the burden off others? You have what it takes. What is needed is for you to know you can make a difference and then reach out to groups who can put those talents to good use. There is never a lack of need for your generosity. What seems to be out of your comfort zone just might be what is needed in your life to rise to a higher calling.

October 10

Affirmation: Today I will pass it along.

In my town there is an organization called Pass It Along. It is a group of adults and teens who plan events and do hands-on activities to make the community better. Their premise is that they can only thank you for what you have done by helping someone else out. The success is overwhelming. Children and teens benefit from helping others. Adults and children bond at a common level.

In other communities, there are groups that gather for a community garden or join walkathons. Children donate their hair to those in need and have bake sales and lemonade stands to raise money for those who are less fortunate. The overwhelming success of giving back is undeniable. If you ask someone who participates in giving back, you will hear that giving is far more rewarding and fulfilling than receiving.

Find out what you have to give, and start giving back. You will be amazed at how your life changes for the better. You're doing God's work whenever you help others along. When you give, you receive.

October 11

Affirmation: I have what I need, and I am grateful.

I have everything I need. I'm blessed. There are times when this simple fact is overlooked, and I think there are so many things that I want that I can't have. If you are like me, you start comparing yourself to others and want what they have instead. Perhaps it's a bigger house, a nicer car, or more money in the bank.

What we don't know or may be unaware of is what they have that we don't want. Perhaps they're going through marital troubles or they have a sick child. To want what others have is to pick and choose, and that's not possible. So instead of looking at what you don't have, focus on the many blessings you do have.

The most important thing when thinking about what you have is not to focus on the monetary things in life. Do you have friends who care about you? Do you have a loving family? Are you healthy? These are the things that matter, and only you can be happy with what you've got.

If you always want what you can't have, think about what's missing in your life. Look around. Is there anything in life that would make your life better? Are you able to get that for yourself? If the answer is yes, then by all means add to your life what you feel is missing.

In life we make concessions. Making adjustments or sacrifices is never a bad thing. Being where you want to be is putting the pieces of the puzzle together. What you have now may not be what you need later on in life. It's a constant reorganization of the priorities in life. I hope you are where you want to be. Nothing is more important.

October 12

Affirmation: What lies within me is love.

Start the day off with a heart full of love. Look for every opportunity to increase the love in your life. What's inside you guides whatever it is you're doing, whatever intentions you have, and however you're feeling at any given moment. Hatred, animosity, and jealousy can also guide your life. What will you choose? Are you the person who wakes up with love in your heart and aspirations for an amazing day, but it soon turns out that you find yourself upset and angry? What happened?

What tends to happen in a day that starts off well is that somewhere along the line core intention is let go. Perhaps breakfast is missed, you may end up in traffic, and, rather than taking the time to listen to a good book on tape or think about the fun you're going to have on the weekend, you find yourself upset with the car that's speeding or the person in the other lane who won't let you in. Where's the love? Try taking account of when you are feeling less than amazing. What is going on? Take a moment to give yourself time to get back the internal feeling of what makes you happy and what promotes the best general feeling of all.

October 13

Affirmation: I will live in the moment today, whether it is or isn't completely perfect.

Are you okay with your life? The key to a happy life is not to strive for perfection but rather to work toward being good enough. Strive to be a good-enough friend, a good-enough parent, and a good-enough employee. Then and only then can we take flight and soar. When my children were young, I never expected or taught them about perfection. The concept was not in our vernacular. Today all three of my children are exceptional in their chosen fields and in their lives. They started out as good-enough students, good-enough friends, and good-enough kids. Where they wanted to go further, they did. They followed where their talents, desires, and passions took them. Are they perfect in every way? They are to me.

Doing what is not expected of you with an open heart is giving back. A random act of kindness is a selfless act performed by a person wishing either to assist or to cheer someone up. Practice kindness and acts of selflessness. It will propel you away from perfectionism and into greatness.

October 14

Affirmation: I am the only person I can change.

We have our own rhythms. For some it's faster, and for some it's slower. When you are forced to live outside your own rhythm, it's exhausting. Remember to keep coming back to your rhythm.

Often we find ourselves overworked, overstressed, and overwrought. Some people continue on at a pace that does not feel right for them. They push themselves beyond their limits. How many times have you found yourself in a position where you just want to take a rest and regroup or go home and put your feet up, but, because of extraneous circumstances, that is not possible? When you have a "normal" day, you are able to take things in stride, but the opposite can happen. You have a setback, and you are feeling low, out of sorts, or depressed. Do not allow yourself to suffer from inertia. Don't allow yourself to stay at rest when you know the best thing for you to do is to get up and take a walk, go to the gym, or simply begin work on the project you have been putting off. Personally, I go from one extreme to the other, but I have found that pacing myself is the healthiest position for me to take. In doing so, I have to know my strengths, weaknesses, and personal boundaries. The next step is to follow through. You will be happy you did.

October 15

Today I will start something new and exciting.

When you start something new—a project or even a career—more than likely you will focus on the flaws or what you are doing wrong. When one focuses on the imperfections in the beginning, he or she will lose heart and give up. People who have accomplished greatness, mastered their craft, or are outstanding in their field will tell you about failed attempts, missed opportunities, and trials and tribulations of seeing the task to fruition and the multiple times they felt like quitting. Building the pyramids didn't happen over night, and many lives were lost. Try whatever speaks to you. What did you want to do as a child? Did you dance a lot? Play with clay? Want to be a firefighter? Talk to the seven-year-old you, your inner child, get back in touch with what it is that you always wanted to do, and give it a try. If you start something new, please recognize that you don't have to be the best all the time; however, it is important to do your best and have fun.

October 16

Affirmation: When I am angry, I will let go of the need to be right.

Anger, hurt, and resentment are emotions generally saved for the people you are closest to, but not always. Sometimes we take our anger out on complete strangers. When we feel hurt, slighted, or wronged, our natural tendency is to get angry or lash out. When we are angry, we no longer feel connected in a loving way. Because we are no longer communicating positively, we shout to be heard. The less we are heard, the louder we get and the more resentful and frustrated we feel. The angrier we get, the louder we shout. Anger is an innate emotion, as are fear, happiness, and sadness.

Of course, we can "hear" someone who is yelling at us. Chances are, however, that by this time we have shut down. We focus only on our feelings and our points of view. This leads to the other person getting more and more indignant. That person knows he or she is not being heard, which leads to greater frustration on both sides of the aisle.

What can we do? We can practice fighting fairly, with dignity, mutual respect and love.

October 17

Affirmation: What others think of me is none of my business.

It doesn't matter what people think of you. All that matters is what you think of yourself. People's opinions are driven by their perceptions and their outlook on life. Someone else's opinion of you can be skewed or inaccurate. Someone else's opinion of you can be harmful or hurtful. If, on the other hand, other people think highly of you and give you praise, it's an added bonus. Accolades and praise keep you on the right track and are necessary for helping boost your self-esteem. However, praise should be accepted but not expected.

What others think of you is irrelevant. Some might focus too much on what others think, to the point they are not living their lives authentically. They find themselves doing only what they think others want them to do. They do only what they think others expect. This can get exhausting. If we care about what others think of us, we will constantly be second-guessing ourselves, and we might eventually give up.

We do our best. We live our lives the way we want to live them. We don't give in to popular opinion. The most important opinion of each of us is our own.

October 18

Affirmation: Boredom is not okay.
Rest and relaxation are.

If you are bored, you are not paying attention. When you start to pay attention to even the most common objects in nature and your immediate surroundings, you open yourself up to the full experience, and a new world begins to present itself. The more your senses and minds are dulled, the more bored and complacent you become. Video games, surfing the web, and reality TV shows are pastimes that are geared toward numbing the senses. They act as an escape into a world that takes you away. There is a time and place for meditative practices and activities that can have a calming effect, such as photography, painting, knitting or reading a good book (my personal favorites).

When you have just about had it and you are at the end of your rope, watching television or going on social media can be harmless and fun. Keep in mind, however, that pleasure-seeking activities provide a temporary euphoria, an escape, and a high, and they come with addictive properties that can get out of hand. Being addicted to knitting sweaters is not necessarily a bad thing, but if you can't stop and it impacts your daily life, you, my friend, just might have to make some adjustments!

October 19

Affirmation: Wisdom begins with wonder.

Do you have, or have you had in the past, a passion for something—anything? Of course you have. When you continue learning and fine-tuning what it is that you love, you will eventually become wise and knowledgeable in that area. Having wisdom and mastery of a subject that excites you brings pure joy.

Whether it is woodworking, physics, painting, or rock climbing, mastery brings with it a sense of purpose. Having a focus and accomplishing that which sets you apart causes you to pause and revel in your achievement. Whatever it is that you are drawn to can provide purpose and a desire to learn and grow.

The next step in mastering a skill is to teach what you have learned to others. Teaching others what you know is a gift to the student but also a gift to yourself. It is said that if you want to be more proficient in an area, teach one person that which you have just learned yourself.

Life is a journey, and continuing education is crucial to living a balanced life. You can become a pianist, sing in a band, or fly-fish if you wish. It is never too late, and it is always your choice to grow.

October 20

Affirmation: I can fight to be right, or I can be at peace.

Be selective in your battles. Sometimes peace is better than being right. Having to be right is ego driven. Who cares if you are right or wrong when you are hurting the ones you love? Why is it so important to be right when you are hurting yourself and possibly destroying relationships? Think about it. Is it worth losing everything to be a "right" fighter?

Let the other person have the last word. The concept of right and wrong is purely individual. We all have different ways of looking at the same thing. Right and wrong is purely about perception. What is right for you might not be right for someone else. The need to get your point across and be validated is futile. Some people will see things your way, and others won't. You can't be right all the time. Therefore, take away the importance of having to think you know it all. Let go of your need to rule. You'll be just fine in the backseat. There will come a time when you are steering the ship. All is well.

October 21

Affirmation: Today I will not take my work home.

Bigger, better, more ... and more! Chances are you, or a loved one, work to the point of exhaustion and are judged by your level of productivity rather than your dedication or professionalism. What one brings to the table is what matters most. There is constant pressure to perform. People are working harder for less. Does this sound familiar? Pressure at work produces stress, feelings of inadequacy, and deep-rooted unhappiness that comes out in other ways. Perhaps you sleep too much on the weekends or have lost interest in things you once enjoyed. Or maybe your family is telling you that you're not the same as you used to be in whatever size, shape, or form that manifests. What can be done?

Channel the stress and anxiety into something positive. When at work, take breaks. Get up from your desk, and stretch every now and then. Take a lunch break. Do not eat in your car! Nothing is so important that you can't take time during the day for yourself. During your commute, do not think of work or the people with whom you work. Let the pressures of the day go. Listen to relaxing music. Take the country road now and then instead of the highway. Focus on transitioning from employee to husband, dad, wife, mom, lover or friend. Let everything go that interferes with being your relaxed, loving self. Let go of the fear of not being good enough, and focus on doing your very best. If you are doing your best, that's good enough.

October 22

Affirmation: I am who I am.

There are introverts and extroverts, those who are outgoing and those who are shy and timid. Most of us fall somewhere in the middle. Why are some people able to walk into a room and be the life of the party, when someone else finds it painful to speak up? You might think that the extrovert is confident, is able to talk to anyone, and command an audience. Did you ever think that the extrovert might be as insecure as the introvert but has a different way of showing it? Have you ever considered that the extrovert acts as if he or she has it all together, when in essence he or she is just as intimidated as anyone else? After the party, the extrovert can walk away and be as hard on himself or herself as the person who remained quiet and reserved. Perhaps the person who was quiet fared better and was better able to cope with the situation because he or she did not feel the need to overcompensate for his or her shortcomings.

Whether you are outgoing, stay mostly to yourself, or find yourself somewhere in the middle, perhaps you are reluctant to let others see the inner light that identifies you as unique. You may limit what you share with others. You may hide your uniqueness. The answers to who, what, when, why, and how about yourself are concealed, constricted, censored, and limited. The introvert keeps his or her answers to himself or herself, and the extrovert hides his or her answers by diverting the spotlight to other people.

So, it seems, we're basically all the same when it comes to revealing ourselves in a healthy and balanced way. Limiting the expression of who you are or living out loud and letting the world know are balancing acts for everyone. Gain and maintain healthy boundaries. It is basically the same for everyone.

October 23

Affirmation: I am happy to share what I know with others.

Nobody has it all, but everybody has something. Everyone has something to share. You have gifts and talents that are unique. What talents do you possess? Are you a good organizer? Are you a good leader? Are you a good teacher? Are you a healer? Are you fluent in more than one language? Whatever it is, are you hiding your talents under a rock or keeping them to yourself for fear of being scrutinized or judged? Are you embarrassed to share the skills that you are proud of and that you love?

When you give of your time and talent, not only are you helping others but you are reaping the rewards of knowing that you are making a difference in someone else's life. The experience and knowledge you have lovingly cultivated over the years are being put to good use. Why keep what is unique about you to yourself? Teach others, and learn from the experience. Learn from your students. Not only will your mind expand, but also your heart and soul will benefit from the blessings of your efforts.

October 24

Affirmation: I take responsibility for my actions.

All actions have reactions. Your actions, good or bad, have consequences. You might be, or you might know or love, a person who does not take responsibility for his or her actions. That person blames others for everything. He or she is unwilling or unable to accept his or her role in any given scenario.

The reality of cause and effect is harsh. Science has proven that what happens naturally has to be real. Not only do people blame others for their role but they do it over and over again. Simply put, actions that get the same results tend to be repeated.

Change happens only if the situation requires change or if you choose to do things differently. When you find yourself being the recipient of someone else not stepping up, refuse to be the target. Set clear and consistent boundaries, and do not let others take their frustrations out on you. Change the routine by breaking the pattern. Refuse to be the one who gets blamed for everything. The person who does not take responsibility for his or her actions does so because that person can. Positive change weeds out failure and makes room for growth.

October 25

Affirmation: I use my time well, thoughtfully, and lovingly.

How many moments do you miss in a day? How many days do you squander in a week? How many weeks fly by in a year? Are you keenly aware of your time and how you spend it? Are you visiting loved ones, playing with your children, and going to the movies with your partner? Or are you wasting time by letting moments drift away, unaware that you are not living fully or in the present? Are you worried about the future or stuck in the past? Or do you know or love someone who is? Now is the opportune moment to be awake, be aware, and be alive.

You or a loved one might succumb to the battle cry "I'm too tired." Or perhaps "I don't have the money for that." If you heard it once, you've heard it repeatedly. When this is the case, generally speaking, the person is diverting the fact that he or she doesn't want to do the activity or get off the couch for some underlying reason. Perhaps stagnation or depression is lurking under the surface. Perhaps anger is unresolved, and it's difficult or seemingly impossible to motivate yourself to experience joy.

There could be any number of reasons for not participating in life, but the one thing that is certain is that people who feel this way are letting their lives go by unfulfilled. They choose not to be present for their friends, family, or themselves. It helps to look deeper into the reason behind the excuses for not living life to the fullest.

Do something today that is challenging. Do something that goes beyond your comfort zone. A new challenge awaits. It's a new opportunity to shine!

October 26

Affirmation: I possess the traits that I don't necessarily like in others. I can change this.

When you think of a person who irritates you, what is it about that person that bothers you? Think of the first trait that comes to mind that is upsetting to your sensibilities. It may come as a surprise, but that is a quality you possess yourself; it's called "projection." We find these qualities to be offensive, and we repress their existence. We don't acknowledge traits in ourselves that we find objectionable. By denying our negative traits that we so despise in others, we outwardly face the world by putting our best self forward. But it is not our face—it's a game face!

One way of getting to the root of who you really are is a practical one. First, list the qualities you do not like in others. Shorten the list to ones that really push your buttons. These are the negative traits that you have denied for so long. Everyone has a long and short list. We all hide our shortcomings to be able to get beyond our human frailties (no joke).

Next, once you have identified your shortcomings, you are free to get in touch with your weaknesses, you are free to become whole and balanced.

When you are finally comfortable with yourself—warts and all—the results might surprise you. You will find increased energy, because you are no longer fighting your demons and you are no longer worried about being "found out." You become more accepting of others with whom you can readily identity, and you can take your negatives and change them into strengths at will. Take a deep breath, be open, be brave, be strong, and be willing to admit some of those rejected parts of yourself into your awareness. In that ongoing process, become more energized, more at ease, more accepting, more compassionate, more vital, and more loving.

October 27

Affirmation: Today I will finish what I started.

What have you been trying hard to avoid? An uncomfortable feeling within you? A difficult situation? A conflict with someone? A hurt? Or even a chore or a task you've been putting off? Think of all the energy it takes to not do what you don't want to do. Think of how liberating it can be to simply take care of what needs to be done. Maybe you are waiting for someone else to do it for you.

When we avoid the inevitable, anxiety and stress grow to the point of being seemingly overwhelming. When we tackle our demons, they frequently shrink in size. By dealing with that which we most want to avoid, we may recognize more personal strength, power, and love that we have available but simply haven't been aware of. You too may discover that as you face the issue at hand, exactly and completely, you can move on and recognize more positive energy and freedom.

October 28

Affirmation: I am alive. I am here.
I will make the best of it.

You might not think of yourself as a spiritual being. You might not be familiar with what that means. You might think it means religious words, beliefs, and practices. If spirituality is a difficult concept for you to grasp, you are not alone. The body–mind–spirit connection is the essence of this book and, therefore, requires ongoing clarification and thought-provoking dialogue.

Take the time to answer a very basic question: what makes you feel most alive? Your answer is your spirituality! It is about whatever adds deeper meaning and greater authenticity, creating a more mindful and abundant life.

Every moment you have the ability to move from passivity into a more conscious experience of going through the pain to get to peace, going through the darkness to get to light, going through sadness to get to joy, getting through fear to get to love, and going through loss to get to abundance.

October 29

Affirmation: I live my life the way I choose.

You no doubt get opinions from family, friends, and even strangers on how you should live your life. People have no problem giving unsolicited advice when it comes to others. Everyone has an opinion, and they do not hesitate to let you know how they feel. Most people tell you what they wish they had done with their lives, or they might try to live vicariously through you. With all this pressure, you might resist breaking the mold and conform to an expected life. With all the extraneous thoughts and ideas from others, it is difficult to be your authentic self. It is difficult to know who you are at times. The key to success and balance in your life is to be aware that the courage to be oneself consistently comes into play throughout your entire life.

Pressure rises as you continue to seek or maintain your rightful place in life. Living the life you are meant to live comes in the form of testing limits periodically and breaking out and making healthy, well-thought-out choices when you find yourself unhappy or discontented. You must reassess relationships, career choices, educational opportunities, and most importantly your health and wellness (in body, mind, and spirit), all while taking into consideration peer pressure, dysfunctional family dynamics, and self-imposed expectations or limitations. What works at age twenty might not work at age forty. With all the consequences and rewards, it takes courage to grow up. Understand, own, and give life to your unique individuality.

October 30

Affirmation: Today I will pencil in some "me" time.

Instead of having more time to do less and less, you end up having less and less time to do more and more. If this is the case for you, something has to give. Children and families require attention. Work or perhaps kids' activities take up most of your waking hours. You long for a time when it will be time for you—time you can rest and take it easy. The battle cry is "There just aren't enough hours in a day!" A peaceful, quiet, and serene existence is seemingly the exception. You might not get "me" time down the road. You might not get time to relax and enjoy your life later on, because later on never comes. The key is to put you first now.

Regardless of self-imposed schedules and responsibilities ("self-imposed" because you choose what you do and what you don't do), it is important to occasionally slow down, regroup, refocus, and relax. Being overworked and overstressed can lead to feelings of anger, anxiety, and frustration. You might even take your resentment out on others.

Today, look for opportunities to stop, take a few deep breaths, and focus on your wants and needs. Try meditation, going for a walk, listening to music, or reading a book for pleasure. Become aware of when you are spreading yourself too thin. Get into the habit of taking a moment before you begin an activity to center yourself and ask yourself, "Is this in my best interest, or am I doing this out of fear or guilt?" Choose not to operate out of guilt but rather out of love for others and for yourself.

October 31

Affirmation: I give to others what I need most.

When you feel wanted, appreciated, and accepted, you thrive and flourish. In an atmosphere of warmth and caring, you grow and blossom. When kindness and understanding are missing, however, you fail to succeed or prosper. Everyone needs acceptance and longs to feel wanted. Everyone wants to feel heard and understood but at some level find it difficult, almost impossible, to follow the formula of "give to others what you want most." This is a basic psychological and spiritual principle. If you want love, give love.

When you want what you are not getting from the other person, you grow further and further apart. You wait for that person to make the first move. The bigger the gap, the harder it is to come together in a healthy, more loving way. It can be done, however, by developing a greater sense of awareness on your part, time and compassion for yourself and your partner. You have the potential for a new start and a fresh beginning as healing takes place and new opportunities appear. Come to the party as the person you want to be!

November

Homeless Youth Awareness Month

November 1

Affirmation: I have only scratched the surface of my potential.

Whatever situation you find yourself in, whatever your circumstances, now is the right time for you to be better and stronger and live with greater purpose. Amp up your vision of the future for yourself. Crank up the volume on what you know is right and good for you. Reassess you goals and aspirations, and make a plan to do better.

It is time to make a move toward being the best version of you. Get in the game, and go for it. If not now, when? Gather what you need. Find the right people who will support your efforts. Plan your journey, and take the first step. If that step feels right, take another and then another. If your heart is open and your vision is clear, you're on your way to success. Strive to do what it takes to reach your full potential in life. Keep your feet on the ground while shooting for the stars!

November 2

Affirmation: Today I will focus on improving myself.

Just when you think it's as bad as it can get, look around and notice your troubles lifting. Things are looking brighter. If you are aware of the possibilities, if you have hope, a brighter day will dawn and crisis will be averted. Without going through the pain needed to heal, the chances are you'll remain in a bad place longer than necessary.

It just might be as easy as recognizing that the very turbulent times come and go with rapid speed. The aftermath, the way you handle your life as a result, is up to you. Look to the end of the storm.

November 3

Affirmation: I will look for signs of rebirth as a compass.

You are told to take a risk, go with your gut, and live life to the fullest. Life is to be lived with all the risks and dangers. Why? Because the danger you fear might be just that: fear. Worry and anxiety are fear getting in the way of living a full and happy life. Whether it's changing jobs or moving out of the city (or to the city), you are constantly making decisions to step out of your circle and seek what is missing in life.

Change is inevitable. Some people say they hate change, but if you observe nature, the colors, smells, and sights are changing minute to minute. Not wanting to change is simply saying, "I don't want to deal with what happens as a result. I don't want to rock the boat. I'm comfortable as I am." Being comfortable is not always a good thing. Try letting go. Change is going to come.

November 4

Affirmation: I will make room for regret in my life.

Can you think of something in life you regret? Are there times that come to mind when you could have or would have done something differently? What comes to mind for me is when I was not right with someone and treated that person badly. However, I've made peace with my past decisions. I now move forward to the future.

Regret is a negative emotional reaction to past acts and behaviors. If you don't have regrets, you are not being honest, real, or compassionate.

When something in your life is over, the tendency is to react with sadness, anger, or other negative emotions. Regret is just that. It's a negative emotion. To minimize regret, you must live in the moment and make the most of each day. When you act or behave badly, say you are sorry and move on. Fix it. Don't leave the business of forgiveness until later. When you look back and see that you're handling the circumstances in your life the best way you possibly can, *smile.*

November 5

Affirmation: I will try again until I am happy with the results.

One of the hardest things to do in life is to stay the course. Success is measured by the journey. Look at everything it took for you to get here. Was it easy? Did you feel like giving up? Did you stay true to your goal?

When you finish something, whether it is running a marathon or cooking a healthy meal, you feel a sense of accomplishment. No one can take that away from you. You may judge yourself too harshly. Perhaps you beat yourself up at times. You may even give up. But then there are times when, against all odds, you persevere and come out on top. Congratulations to you! Take this pat on the back. It is well deserved.

November 6

Affirmation: I will let go of what is nonessential in my life.

What is it that makes you strive for more in life, while others remain where they are? If you are happy with your life and your situation, there is no need to make great changes. If you are satisfied, the beauty is in recognizing that you are where you are because of hard work and decisions you made that work for you and your family.

However, for those who have more mountains to climb, the measure of achievement is satisfaction. If you are not satisfied with where you are in life, keep moving. Figure it out. Do what it is that you have always wanted to do. Raise the bar. Enlist others who will support you. Gather what you need, and just do it.

November 7

Affirmation: Today I will take time to be still.

Trust yourself to know what to do. All it takes is a quiet moment, a deep breath, and time to find the answers for which you are looking. No one else knows you like you do. You can ask for help or seek advice, but in the end you're your own expert. It's your life.

Quieting our minds is not always easy. It is when we need to take time to consider our options that we are the most frantic. Get up from the desk, and take a walk. Find a meditation room or a quiet corner. Ask yourself the hard questions. The answers will come.

November 8

Affirmation: I will be skeptical of what others have to say.

Not knowing the latest gossip is a good thing. You don't have to know everyone else's business. In the world of social media you are now expected to keep up with everyone's latest hiccup. Be aware of the information you are getting. What's happening is that you now know everything that is not important.

If you are on a social media site, stay alert to the possibilities of getting caught up with posting your every move. Be careful when posting "about you" online. Your private information and photos are up for grabs. You can be judged on what you post and like. It's a bully's playground, and your info can be used against you. When in doubt, leave it out.

November 9

Affirmation: Today I will not give up on my dream.

Never give up on a dream just because of the length of time it will take to achieve it. The time will pass anyway. If you are working on a goal, you will eventually obtain it. If you just sit around and think about it, naturally it will never get done. If you want to go back to school, for example, but discover it will take you three years to complete your studies, that amount of time may seem overwhelming to you. Well, guess what. That time will go by whether you are taking classes or not. If you decide to go for it, you can always change your mind if it is not for you, but you might regret never taking the first step. If you want something bad enough, time should not be a factor at all.

Reaching your goals is not amazing only to you but also to your loved ones, especially your children. They see you as being someone who conquered reservations, who is fearless, and who knows what you want and obtains it. That alone is more precious than the actual decision to chase your dream. Despite the fact that whatever you did is a memory, the fact that you took a chance and turned out a winner remains. Take a chance. Go for the gold. Be a winner.

November 10

Affirmation: Today I will make new mistakes.

This affirmation came from a refrigerator magnet. I absolutely love it. Of all the words of wisdom handed down over generations, I would love to know who is responsible for recognizing that we all make mistakes and all we can do is to try not to make them again! "Failing differently" is the key to a healthy and well-adjusted life. It's said that the definition of *crazy* is doing the same thing twice and expecting different results. Well, how many of us make the same mistake over and over and over again, never realizing that these mistakes have worn out their welcome and that new ones are waiting in the wings. Mistakes are going to happen. We are human, after all. Because of a fear of failure, some of us try never to make mistakes. If you are afraid to fail, you are also afraid to take risks, and as we all know, there is no greatness without risk taking. Decide with your instinct, your heart, and your mind.

November 11

Affirmation: I am beautiful, and so are you.

Mirrors don't lie. The reflection on glass is simply a play between light and shadows. The only true mirror that reflects our self-image and self-worth is the mirror within each of us. Clear your mind of doubt and negativity. Let go of any preconceived notions you have from your past. Think of yourself in a kind and loving way, just for the moment. Now take a long, deep breath. Look at your reflection in the mirror. It's changed! How wonderful you look when you let go and just be who you are in the moment.

If you're afraid of the mirror and don't want to acknowledge your personal beauty, you're not alone. However, not being comfortable with your looks may be an indication of a greater need. Start from this very moment. Let go of past negative thoughts and feelings about yourself. What are you feeling now in this moment? There are concrete steps to finding your inner beauty.

Make peace with your imperfections; everyone has them. Be less judgmental of yourself and others. Smile and look at yourself as others who love you do. When you are in that moment of being right with who you are and what you look like, when the way you look actually makes you feel better about yourself, you will see yourself as God sees you … beautiful.

November 12

Affirmation: Angels are never too distant to hear you.

When I look closely, I can witness angels around me in many forms. It's so difficult at times to see the good through the veiled darkness. When hard times are upon you, you tend only to see the hurt, pain, devastation, fury, and sadness. It's then that you are called upon to balance out the darkness with your inner light. No one expects you to be happy all the time. No one expects you to be happy when you are grieving a loved one or when you witness injustice. The key to balancing negative and positive feelings is to recognize the need to get out of your slump. Enough time for grief has passed. You are being called to rise above. Call on a friend, relative, or counselor who can take some of the pain away by letting you talk openly, averting your attention to something more positive and productive.

Try not to give in to the feelings that are overwhelming and hurtful. What I know to be true is that it's very important to feel the pain of grief and hurt. Feel the pain of devastation and loss. Never try to suppress it or think it will go away if you don't think about it. Trust me—repressing pain comes out in different, more harmful ways. Look to others to ease your pain. There are angels all around you to help with your burdens. Be aware of the angels in your life.

November 13

Affirmation: The opposite of worry is faith.

I have faith in all outcomes for the enrichment and enhancement of the journey. I believe we always know. Our instincts, thoughts, and experiences tell us what we need to do. Let them lead you. You might not think you know what the right thing to do is, but you do know. You might not have all the information you need to make a sound decision. You might not be aware of all your options, but you do know what it is that you want and need. If you don't, who does?

When you call on God for help and don't accept the help of others who are connected to God, you are rejecting help. God works through others. God works through individuals who care.

Loneliness is self-inflicted. It takes making that call or maybe talking to a neighbor to whom you might not otherwise talk. Get to know people in your community through organizations in which you have a shared interest. Loneliness is a result of being hurt by the people you love. However, there is no guarantee regarding who loves us. Therefore, we all must seek out people who need us; we will then find those people who can truly help, make us laugh, and help to get us through good times and bad. It takes being a friend to have a friend. Say to yourself, "Today I will reach out to three people." It's so vital for us, as human beings, to treat others as we want to be treated, to love when it's not easy, and to be the kind of people with whom we most want to be.

November 14

Affirmation: Today I will attempt to right the wrongs in my life.

Surrendering is not giving up; it is knowing when we've had enough. When we let go and let God, we are surrendering. We are giving up control and our need to be right. To many, the word *surrender* is not a good thing. We equate surrendering with giving up, losing, and negativity. For many of us it is difficult to surrender emotionally; the thought of letting go goes against every fiber of our beings. Letting go is *not* giving up.

Letting go can lead to a spiritual awakening. When a spiritual awakening happens, it throws us off balance and forces us to readjust, reinvent ourselves, and look at the world and our relationships in a different, more loving, and positive way. It forces us to assess what's wrong in our lives and take the necessary steps to make it right. You may not even know something is not working in your life, but trust me—others are aware, and so is the universe.

November 15

Affirmation: Today I will be more caring.

Entropy, atrophy, and apathy are contagious. "Entropy" is how scientists measure the degree of disorder present in a system. "Atrophy" is a term used in the medical profession to define the loss of mass and strength causing prolonged immobility, possibly caused by being at rest too long. "Apathy" is a lack of feeling, emotion, interest, and concern. It is a mental state of not caring or having lack of interest in emotional, spiritual, or physical life. Apathetic people just don't care anymore. Indifference or the suppression of emotions, such as passion, excitement, motivation, or concern, leads to disorder and immobility. So it appears that entropy + atrophy = apathy. It is the absence of interest in or concern about your own philosophical, emotional, spiritual, social, psychological, and physical health and wellness or that of others.

The solution is to try to find meaning and purpose in your life. If you have a positive outlook and for now know all is well, perhaps you can be there for someone who is sluggish and down and perhaps doesn't have the tools needed to confront his or her demons. Not caring or being insensitive to others can be a learned behavior, which means it can also be unlearned.

November 16

Affirmation: Today I will define exactly what my peace is.

For some, or perhaps for most, peace is elusive. During very stressful periods in our lives we might not find any peace. Perhaps you have forgotten what peace really feels like. My peace comes when my life, job, home, and activities are not demanding anything of me at the moment and all is well outwardly. My peace comes when I'm not experiencing strife with my friends or colleagues. My peace is when my family members are healthy and doing well in their lives. My peace comes when I'm healthy, feeling happy to be alive, and feeling that where I am is where I need to be. Define peace for yourself, and watch everything fall into place.

November 17

Affirmation: Today I will call a friend to walk with me.

Children are always running ahead or trying to keep up. Perhaps you're the one who always has to be the leader, or you're one of those people who are happy to follow. It doesn't have to be an "either/or" thing." You can walk together. Take your time. Enjoy the stroll and the conversation. Experience the feeling of "I am there for you, and you are here for me." It doesn't get much better than that.

November 18

Affirmation: I will recognize when I am in a rut.

You may be too young to think of the "autumn" of your life. If that is the case, perhaps you can relate to a loved one who can. If you can relate to the "autumn years," shake it up a bit. Try to look ahead, and do what it takes not to let life pass you by. If you are single and want to find someone to spend your life with, look for a mate. If you want to be healthy and fit, eat healthfully and exercise. Complacency is giving up. It's living in a rut. Sitting on the couch and eating your meals in front of the television are common forms of complacency. They can be symptoms of giving up on love. They can be signs of giving up on yourself.

November 19

Affirmation: Today I will see an opportunity in every difficulty.

When an opportunity comes your way, are you excited to take on the challenge? You have the prerogative to turn it down or reverse your decision whenever it's not working out. If there's no chance that you can give it up, you might be hesitant to take on whatever the opportunity might be. The word *opportunity* tells you that an exciting moment is ahead of you, designed for you. It is a chance that you might not otherwise get with your name on it. Be grateful. Be excited. Weigh the pros and cons. When opportunity knocks, you answer.

November 20

Affirmation: Thank you, thank you, thank you.

I am grateful, not only for the good things in my life but also for the not-so-good things. Things with which I struggle the most make me who I am. It's easy to be grateful for the things that make you happy. Turn your thoughts to the events, circumstances, and people that make your life difficult.

We all must live with pain and sorrow. Hopefully, we all experience our fair share of happiness and joy as well. When things go wrong for you, use the opportunity to call to mind all that is going right in your life. Focusing on, and being thankful for what is working in your life has the power to make the rough patches a bit smoother. If you never experience negativity, harm, and pain, you will not know joy.

What about the joy in your life? How often do you stop to be truly thankful for those around you who are making your life just a little bit easier? Thank a teacher, a friend, or a parent. Do you stop to tell those whom you love that you are grateful for their encouragement? That you are thankful they have stood by you in good times and in bad? Do you let yourself know how grateful you are for the fortunes in your life? Or are you preoccupied with the trouble you experience?

The most important lesson in life is to appreciate others and yourself. Be grateful for your blessings. Be grateful for the situations in which you find yourself and the situations, for whatever reason, you have escaped. Take a moment to list all the people, things, and experiences for which you are most grateful. Do this daily in a gratitude journal. It will lift your mood and your spirits. The power of knowing what your blessings are and where they come from is restorative. Be honest. Be aware. Be grateful.

November 21

Affirmation: My work and words are for the good of others.

Have you found your mission in life? Have you ever thought of what you do as your mission? Does what you do for a living make the world a better place? Is providing for your family helping others, as well? Do you give of your time and talents to your community and to those less fortunate? If so, you can rest at night, knowing you are working for a common good. Is what you have to say positive and uplifting all or most of the time? Make an effort to be someone who makes a difference. Helping others is a mission in life for us all.

November 22

Affirmation: Today I will stay away from people who are not good for me.

What does it mean to have people in your life who make you feel alone? Were there times in your life when you were in a relationship with someone who thought only of himself or herself? Were there people who made you feel bad by the way they treated you or the way they talked to you? If this is not your experience, do you know someone who might be going down this path in life?

Perhaps you were a victim of being treated badly. My wish for you is that, if you are with anyone who makes you feel alone, you recognize your self-worth and self-importance and get very far away. It doesn't have to be a significant other; it can be a boss or colleague who makes you feel alone. You can break away and make changes for the better with help. You don't have to put up with what is not beneficial to you. You deserve to be appreciated.

November 23

Affirmation: I can fight to be right, or I can be at peace.

Be selective in your battles. Sometimes peace is better than being right. Having to be right is ego driven. Who cares if you are right or wrong when you are hurting the ones you love? Why is it so important to be right when you are hurting yourself and possibly destroying relationships? Think about it. Is it worth losing everything to be a "right" fighter?

Let the other person have the last word. The concept of right and wrong is purely individual. We all have different ways of looking at the same thing. Right and wrong is purely about perception. What is right for you might not be right for someone else. The need to get your point across and be validated is futile. Some people will see things your way, and others won't. You can't be right all the time. Therefore, take away the importance of having to think you know it all. Let go of your need to rule. You'll be just fine in the backseat. There will come a time when you are steering the ship. All is well.

November 24

Affirmation: Today I will try to be more empathetic.

Standing in someone else's shoes means that you put yourself in that person's position and think long and hard about how you would act or react in a similar situation. Given the same set of circumstances, you might do the same thing. Chances are, unless you have a very close relationship with a person or you share a similar bond, you probably have little to no idea what someone else is thinking or feeling or why they do what they do. This is where empathy comes in. You might not know exactly what is going on in someone else's life, but you can share the feelings of another and cultivate the ability to understand.

Some folks have hardened their hearts and don't care about or are not sensitive to the needs of others. They lack compassion. Closed minds and those who shut others out are dismissive at best. Labeling, teasing, and bullying others because they are different leads to aggression.

Who really wants to fight? I have yet to meet anyone who flourishes and grows from anger and bigotry. People are set in their ways, because they find it difficult to change or they don't know how to begin to change. Perhaps they have not been shown compassion or have not been treated fairly, so they become unwilling or unable to show respect to others. They take their feelings of inadequacy out on people they don't even know or people they don't want to get to know.

When you are on the receiving end of being tormented for being different, when you are the one being bullied, or when people are biased against you, you can either suppress the anger or let it go and have compassion for your aggressor. It is not easy, but with time and talking it out with people who know what you are going through, you will possibly end up better for it.

November 25

Affirmation: Know peace, know happiness. No peace, no happiness.

I firmly believe that you can't be happy if you are not at peace. Happiness comes in that brief moment (or moments) when everything is as it should be in your life—for example, when you are in the right place at the right time; when you are with people who love you and support you or when you are working in an environment that promotes your achievements and makes you feel like you are making a difference. When you are providing security for your family, when you have friends who care about you, or when you are at a place in your life that fills you with pride, you can pause and experience an overall feeling of being peaceful and happy in the moment. If you are fortunate to be in good health; or when you are not healthy, but you are supported by a team of experts who are working on your behalf to make you whole again, you can rest assured. Happiness is peaceful, joyful and reassuring. Have a happy day!

November 26

Affirmation: I will remain calm and peaceful today.

You can be calm and peaceful in a field of wildflowers. You can be calm and peaceful on the shoreline. But can you be peaceful in the midst of a storm? Are you calm when your children are running around the house and you have to cook? Are you at peace when you are on a conference call and you are getting nothing but resistance and hostility?

In any given moment, any one of us can be in a less-than-peaceful place. We might hyperventilate or get uneasy. We might find it easy to fly off the handle, usually at those whom we love and who have nothing to do with our current state.

So do you want to get more things accomplished at work? Do you want to have more loving and supportive relationships with your friends and family? Knowing how to remain calm is a key to success. Know that nothing can upset you or prevent you from accomplishing your goal. Some common techniques that have proven to be effective are exercising, eating healthfully, and praying or meditating. None of us can go it alone. Remember—it is helpful to talk out your troubles and fears. Let go, and be successful. Let go, and stay calm.

November 27

Affirmation: Today I will be aware of the beauty in my surroundings.

I love to be wowed by people, nature, animals, and most living and breathing things. What truly excites me is the joy of children when they play together, their little voices, and their laughter. The colors of the sky, the mountains, and a field of wildflowers wow me. I am wowed when I look at my child and witness the love and devotion we have for each other. That's so cliché—corny, you might even think. But it is just this attitude that may keep you from being present with what is around you on a daily basis—life's gifts that you may take for granted. I know that when I walk outside today, I can find one or many things that wow me. Being wowed is from God. Being wowed is being in a peaceful state so that our minds are receptive. I wish you peace and beauty. Peace is always beautiful.

November 28

Affirmation: I will remember that the holidays are for love, peace, and kindness.

When you are at the mall, holiday shopping, and you begin to get frustrated and upset with the number of things you have to do, remember to go home and love your family. When you are at work and you know you have end-of-the-year deadlines and you are way behind, remember to go home and love your family. When everything is falling apart because you have to be with family or friends of whom you want no part, send them love. Focus on what matters. Tinsel, lights, and gifts are all superficial and don't last. No one remembers what you did or didn't do last year. They do remember how you made them feel. Were you open and honest without hurting anyone? Did you provide hospitality and friendship? Take time to be with your faith-based community. Give to others. Teach them love by example. It starts with each one of us, and it continues on to those we teach by our actions, hopes, dreams, and desires. Desire to be even more of a loving person. Care for one another. Love a lot.

November 29

Affirmation: Today I am in a good place. I have let go of animosity, hatred, and jealousy.

Hatred is often associated with feelings of anger, disgust, and hostility. Hatred is deep and emotionally crippling. In this season, it is crucial to take the time to look at what you may hate and how often you may speak your hate. You might not even be aware of what you're projecting. Is hating someone worth your time and effort? Why take the time and effort to direct your energy in such a demeaning and unproductive way? Hatred perpetuates hatred. It is time to stop such animosity.

Jealousy, on the other hand, refers to thoughts and feelings of insecurity, fear, and anxiety. Jealousy consists of emotions such as anger, resentment, inadequacy, helplessness, and disgust. When you are jealous, you have envy in your heart. That is not good for you and not good for the people around you. Look at whom you are jealous of. We generally are not jealous of anything other than individuals. So take a heartfelt inventory of your relationships and the people you feel envy toward. Write down everything and everyone you are thankful for. That is the formula for success.

November 30

Affirmation: When I am alone in nature I feel happy.

Unfortunately, going outside is no longer part of many people's everyday life. Times have changed. The environment may not be as safe as it once was. There may be more obstacles to watch out for and be cautious of. There are precautions to take, and safety comes first. However, there is nothing like a walk outside for our physical and emotional health. The sound of the wind through the trees is joyous. The sparkle of light glistening on a snow-covered tree or the colors of a mountain vista in the autumn is healing to the soul. Take time, even a few minutes a day, to commune with nature. Don't wait until you are on vacation to have fun in the sun. Make it a part of your everyday routine. Breathe the air, feel the sun, listen to the stillness, and be one with the world. Feel what is greater than you, greater than us all.

December

Universal Human Rights Month

December 1

Affirmation: Generosity makes us rich.

If you're feeling poor in riches or poor in spirit, one thing you can do is give something away; give of your time and talents. Instead of focusing on what you don't have, focus on what you do have and how you can bless others with it.

There is a worldwide, nationwide, and local crisis of people desperately in need of food, shelter, and safety. Unfortunately, their voices aren't always heard, and they are not receiving the services and provisions they so desperately need. Basic human needs are not being met because of the enormity of situations throughout the world. Even our servicemen and servicewomen are not getting the services they require and need your help.

What can you do to help others in need? Volunteer at a local food pantry or soup kitchen. Join a church group or an organization that provides services to others. Be a role model for future generations. Giving works wonders when you are in need of a spiritual lift. Giving is divine, and you are being called to do unto others …

December 2

Affirmation: Today I will accept my life the way it is.

Accepting ourselves as we are is a tall order. We cannot change without first accepting our flaws, shortcomings, and weaknesses. Being a little hard on ourselves at times is fine and even normal, but taking it to the extreme of self-loathing condemns us to a life of heartache and tears. It is oppressive and offensive to our senses.

Accepting the people we love is critical. Accepting people from all walks of life, every creed, and every color is crucial and can be much more difficult. The more we try to change someone's viewpoint, belief system, or personal qualities or attributes, the more fragile the relationship can become. We can educate and try our best to help, but we cannot expect to have our own way when it comes to other people. The best way change comes about is if all parties involved want to change. It is difficult to get a loved one to be healthier in body, mind, and spirit. All you can do is your part to help.

When frustration sets in, it is possible and even probable that you can become abrasive. You may consider possibly leaving or giving up on the relationship. You must decide whether or not the person you love means more to you than his or her shortcomings. What you once loved in your partner perhaps you now detest. What is your next strategy? You've run out of ideas.

Accept your loved one for who he or she is right now. Try working on how you react instead of how that person behaves, as long as he or she is not hurting you, hurting others, or hurting a child in any way. If that person is self-destructive and out of control, you can always walk away and get help to improve the situation. Change is good, but only in a loving, caring, and supportive way for the good of the other's spiritual, emotional, and physical health and wellness. If you want to change anyone or anything in your life, first have the confidence and the courage to change yourself.

December 3

Affirmation: Today I will change my thinking so that I can feel differently.

Your emotions are a direct result of how and what you think about what you've said or done. If you think the world is an awful place and you harbor hatred in your heart, you will suffer as a result. You might not recognize it now, but if there is someone in your family or circle of friends who you no longer talk to because of unresolved issues or feelings of anger and resentment, the animosity you feel will ultimately affect your life in negative ways.

For example, you might think that, because that person is no longer in your life, he or she can't hurt you anymore. You might think you must let go of that person because he or she was toxic and brought you nothing but pain. If that is the case, chances are you and the other person did not resolve the situation that brought you to the point of estrangement. Unresolved issues can come back to haunt you, because they are just that, unresolved. Let go of the negativity, and change the way you think about what is actually going on.

Personal growth comes when you recognize the signs that tell you to lighten up, let it go and get it together before it's too late. Perhaps it won't be comfortable at first to change your way of thinking, or it might not make sense to you. Perhaps it doesn't feel genuine to think of the stress in your life as something you can live without if you begin to think differently. If you are open to the possibility of change, you can turn your life around, and the lives of those around you will be affected in a positive way. Taking a personal inventory, thinking it through, and not being sedentary in our emotional or spiritual life are an ongoing process.

December 4

Affirmation: I will be skeptical of what others have to say.

What's happening in our culture, with the onset of social media and search engines, is that we now have as much useless information at our disposal as we have important facts and information. It can be highly distracting and hard to decipher what it is you really want know to know and what you need to know on a daily basis!

Stay alert to the possibilities of getting caught up with posting your every move on social media. Be careful when posting your personal information online. Your private information and photos are up for grabs. You can be judged on what you post and how you interact with others. The Internet is a bully's playground, and your info can be used against you. When in doubt, delete or refrain from posting what doesn't feel right to you.

Social media, however, can be a help in some cases. If you see a friend who is posting negative or hostile comments, be aware that there might be an underlying problem. Studies show that negativity on social media can lead to physical health problems if not regulated. There is good and healthy information to be had on the computer. Social media was designed as a tool to be in touch and to be informed. Use it wisely and with discretion.

December 5

Affirmation: I will do my best and be my best today. I am inspired.

What does it mean to be inspired? Inspiration comes from many sources. Who inspires you? Do feelings, sights, or sounds move you? People, places, and things can inspire you. Words are inspiring.

When you encounter beauty and joy throughout your day, you may be inspired to incorporate a portion of that inspiration into your own life. Whatever moves you inspires you. It is an opportunity to look at your life and recognize what areas can benefit from growth or change.

Or if you know someone who has made great strides in his or her profession, family life, or even physicality, you might be inspired to do the same, because if that person can do it, what is holding you back? Teachers, mentors, parents, friends, and siblings can be sources of inspiration. It is my intention that the words on these pages inspire you. A hunger for knowledge and insight and a true desire to do better are needed to act on the inspiration that you are experiencing. However, you don't always have to change when inspired. Simply being in the presence of a beautiful painting or hearing a lovely song can inspire you in many ways. Ask yourself, "When was the last time I truly was amazed and inspired?"

Today, look for opportunities to be inspired and to be inspirational to others. When you feel joy and your soul is touched, be certain to let that person know the impact he or she had on you. Show up, and be inspired. Show up, and inspire others.

December 6

Affirmation: I trust myself.

Trust your instincts. Sounds pretty basic, right? Sounds simple? For many people it's one of the hardest concepts to grasp and to live by. There are many reasons you second-guess yourself. Perhaps you are afraid to try new things for fear of failure. Or maybe you have a hard time making a decision when other people are involved. When it is scary or even paralyzing to decide, you might look to others to make your decisions for you or choose not to decide and avoid the situation altogether. If you have low self-esteem or anxiety or lack confidence in yourself, chances are that you look to others for answers.

Trust your ability to make clear, well-thought-out, and sound decisions. Most decisions can be reversed if necessary. If you make a decision and want to change it at any time, do not hesitate to do so if possible. If not, then accept the outcome, and move on. The more decisions you make on your own, the easier they will start to become. Right or wrong, it is up to you to decide what is best for you and those you love.

December 7

Affirmation: Today I will go with the flow.

Change happens. Change is necessary. Change is inevitable. If that's the case, why do people fear change so much? Going with the flow is easy for some. Others find it extremely difficult to keep quiet and not rock the boat. Are you a person who can go with the flow, or do you have a need to speak out even when it isn't in your best interest?

Anger and fear are driving forces in preventing the natural flow. When you are angry, fearful, or resentful, you don't want anything in your life to change, for fear of the unknown. Fear of success also can be crippling and prevent you from letting things play out as they should. Fear of happiness might sound ridiculous, but for some, letting go of negativity and pain can be a daunting task. Some people thrive on chaos.

When you find yourself trying to control everything and everyone, take a step back. Let go of the need to control just this one time. Have faith, and trust that things will go as they should. Shift happens.

December 8

Affirmation: I will always believe my life is worth celebrating.

So often we hear people say things like "It's my birthday, but I hate birthdays. It's just another day," or "I don't want to make a big deal out of the holidays." And let's not forget the most resounding battle cry: "I hate the holidays!" At times in my life I have been guilty of wanting the whole holiday season to be over before it even began. Self-imposed pressure, self-inflicted comparisons to others, and feelings of having to be better than "good enough" all lead to emotional meltdowns. For anyone with low self-esteem or for those who just don't feel good about themselves, the holidays can be anything but joyous. If you can rid yourself of expectations altogether or, better yet, have no expectations of others, those around you will be pleasantly surprised. You can have joy and happiness.

December 9

Affirmation: Everything I need comes to me at the perfect time.

Time and patience are needed when waiting for the answer to a prayer. Worrying only produces anxiety and depression. Not having what you want when you want it can cause disappointment and doubt. Not having things go your way can produce frustration, inner turmoil, and even anger. The antidote, the opposite of worrying, is faith and a belief that things will work out as they should.

Worrying is a bad habit. Worrying is wasted time and energy. Worrying produces negativity that comes out in other ways, such as non-productivity, unhappiness, or an ill temperament. How many times have you heard, "You're going to worry yourself sick"?

Peace and contentment come with knowing "all good things come to those who wait." Trust in spirit. Trust in the goodness of your environment, friends, and family. And trust in the power of believing in all that is good. Keep the faith.

December 10

Affirmation: My feelings will not overpower me today.

Good or bad emotions can produce joy or sadness, happiness or pain. Today, the key to happiness is to strike a balance with your emotions. You can always balance your emotions with your thoughts. Change the way you think, and you change the way you feel. Emotions can be deceiving. Emotions lie. Thoughts are concrete and have the power to change the moment, the day, and even your future.

What do you think of when you look to the future? Do you think of happiness and prosperity ahead for you, or are you afraid of losing it all and not being able to handle what the future holds? When you think of the past, do you remember the good times when you were with family and friends and things were simpler, or are you embarrassed or ashamed about what you could or should have done?

Let me reiterate, because it bears repeating. All you have is now! Blink your eyes, and that moment is gone and another one has taken its place. Before you know it, a lot of moments will begin to add up. Unless you choose joy, you might look back with regret, and I know you don't want that.

December 11

Affirmation: Today I will forgive myself.

How many times have you heard, "I can forgive but I can't forget"? This is not true forgiveness. It is a first step, however. Forgiveness is not punishing a person for something he or she has done; it is pardoning that person for being human.

It is only when the thoughts of the offense against you no longer weigh heavily on your mind that you have truly accepted the divine gift of forgiveness in your heart. When you forgive but do not forget, you are hanging onto pain. You aren't forgetting, because possibly you are not ready to let go of the hurt. You are not able to forgive, because you don't trust that the person will not hurt you again. You are afraid that he or she will repeat the offense against you, and you can't handle that.

True forgiveness is giving pardon to your offender, letting go of the negativity, and trusting that your forgiveness has the power to release that person in order for him or her to move on. Not letting go only perpetuates guilt, not only for them but for you, as well. When you are unforgiving, you are not being true to who you are, who you know deep inside as a loving and caring person. By not forgiving and hanging onto anger, you allow that person to remain in control of you, by holding your emotions hostage. That person remains in power and continues to have control over you. What is best for you is to come to the realization that letting go of anger, pain, and resentment can free you to give to others in an unobstructed way. You are now free to give of yourself with an open heart. Please remember that forgiveness is a gift, not only to those who have harmed us but more importantly to yourself and those who love you.

December 12

Affirmation: I am confident. I got this!

Summon self-confidence from your authentic self. Self-confidence equals courage, self-assurance, and self-awareness. You know yourself, and at times you even love yourself.

You got this! Whether or not you were told by your parents, teachers, family, or friends in your past that you are loved, beautiful, capable, and valuable, that little voice inside your head wants you to know that you are, in fact, amazing. You are a good person, yet you still might seek approval and validation from others.

You may desperately seek approval when the only approval you will ever need comes from yourself—being okay with who you are, spending time with yourself, and not being afraid or feeling alone. Everything is okay. You are okay right now. Your dreams and desires come from a good place; your intentions are pure, simple, and basic. You might not always make the best choices in life, but if your intentions are pure and honest you can have peace, knowing that you are doing your best. That is all anyone can ever hope for.

December 13

Affirmation: For today I will say good-bye to the pain in my life.

When we lose a loved one (and we all will), they are no longer here on earth, but we are here to carry on. The person who is no longer with us can no longer see, hear, feel, smell, or taste, but we can carry on the memories we have of when that person was alive. If you're separated or estranged from a friend, parent, spouse, loved one, or anyone near and dear to you, you may feel the void or emptiness that is similar to loss or grief.

The stages of grief are denial, bargaining, anger, acceptance, and moving on. When experiencing grief we are called to rise above at a pace that works for each person individually. It is not a race, and there is no one-size-fits-all time frame. Call on a friend, relative, or counselor who can provide solace and understanding. Sometimes averting your attention to something more positive or productive might help. Try not to give into the feelings that are overwhelming and hurtful. What I know to be true is that it's important to feel the pain of grief and loss.

Your goal in life is to be at peace and be content. Happiness is your birthright. Eastern philosophy has taught us that without pain there can be no joy. Suffer if you must, and then let go, just for today.

December 14

Affirmation: In every difficulty, there is opportunity.

A pessimist sees difficulty in every opportunity. A person who is on the path to being balanced in body, mind, and spirit must choose to see an opportunity for growth in every difficulty.

When an opportunity comes my way, I am excited to take on the challenge. I have the prerogative to turn it down or reverse my decision whenever it's not working out. If there's no chance that I can give it up, I might not take it on, whatever the opportunity might be. The word *opportunity* is telling you that a possible advantageous moment is ahead of you, designed for you; it is a chance that you might not otherwise get, stamped with your name on it. Be grateful. Be excited. Weigh the pros and cons, and then make a decision that works for you.

Many people proclaim they are indecisive. They have trouble making up their minds. I really don't get why a person who is smart and vital and has it seemingly all together cannot make up his or her mind to choose door number one, door number two, or door number three. I know that indecision stems from fear of the unknown and the inability to trust yourself or others.

Make up your mind for your benefit and the well-being of the people in your life. This is the moment when you get to put your faith in yourself, and I suggest putting your source of energy to the test. We all are tested every day. The decisions we are called on to make are too many to fathom. When you are called on to decide, take an educated and calculated risk. Be thoughtful and mindful. You can always turn your ship around.

December 15

Affirmation: Today I relinquish my desire to control others.

When love rules, there is no need to control others. When power predominates, then love is lacking. One is the shadow of the other. *Power* is a word that some people think of fondly and others don't. It depends on how power is used. In relationships with those you love, power over one another has no place. Trying to one-up each other or prove the other person wrong in a controlling manner is not conducive to fostering a loving relationship. Both people end up hurting when the stronger-willed person dominates the less aggressive one. When you think of having power over your children, that too is a losing proposition. Power is turned off and on with the flip of a switch. I suggest, instead of wanting to be powerful, strive for successful, caring, and loving.

Being successful (not vengeful), being constructive (not destructive), and leading with kindness and sincerity are the antidotes to bullying or destructive behavior. You are picked on or taken advantage of when you are perceived to be the weaker of the two. Improve your self-esteem, sense of self, and confidence before, not after, the bully walks through the door. Be on your guard to be on the offensive and not the defensive.

December 16

Affirmation: My thoughts are my destiny.

How you think is how you feel, which is how you act. Thinking clearly and consciously determines your future. You tend to think negatively in any given situation, because studies show that it is more common for you to think the worst than it is to see a brighter side of life. That's because you must be prepared for danger. You must protect your family from what could happen and what danger is possible. Not only is being happy and positive *all* the time abnormal, but it is also truly not in your best interest. Balance between what can possibly go wrong and focusing on the positive can put you in a better position to be able to cope. Being positive is a coping skill that is quite powerful. Whether you are faced with a life-threatening situation or you are making everyday life choices, be aware that there is a time and place for negativity. But when you have the opportunity to be positive, strive to be the light in the darkness.

December 17

Affirmation: My words and deeds are for the good of others.

Have you found your mission in life? Have you ever thought of the work you do as your mission? Does what you do for a living make the world a better place? Is providing for your family helping others, as well? Do you give of your time and talent to your community and those less fortunate? If so, you can rest at night, knowing you are working for a common good.

Ask yourself if what you have to say is positive and uplifting all the time or at least most of the time. Are your words constructive or destructive? Do you lift people up or bring them down? Are you contributing to or contaminating the situation? Make an effort to be someone who makes a difference more often than not. Do you say kind and encouraging words meant to benefit others? Do you make people feel appreciated and wanted? Whatever you are on this planet to achieve, whatever mountains you must climb, you are here to help others help themselves. Happiness comes when your words and deeds make someone else better.

December 18

Affirmation: I will reach out my hand in kindness.

Do you have people in your life that make you feel safe? Are there times in your life when you know that you feel secure and that there are others on your side? Is it a parent, a partner or a friend? Is it a family member, counselor or clergy? We all need someone who has our best interest at heart. Someone who makes us feel better by the way they talk and how they make us feel.

Waking up in the morning and going to sleep at night with the comfort of knowing you have people on your side, people who genuinely care about you and will be there no matter what, is a blessing. My wish for you is that you never feel alone. We all deserve to be appreciated and accepted.

Perhaps you are that person for someone else. If you know someone who you think is alone and could use a friend, today is a great day to reach out to that person. Start a friendly conversation and be supportive of his or her plight. Help out as much as possible; check in now and then. Assist in any way you can. Give of yourself to a group or cause that is near and dear to your heart. If you are in a position to be of assistance, give a little or as much as you can. It does a body, mind, and spirit good.

December 19

Affirmation: I do my best.

Some people always want to be the winner. If they aren't winning, they are not having fun. There are times when it is fun to win the trophy; the ribbon; the prize. We work very hard to achieve our goals in life. There are other times, however, when we must take a step back and be okay with coming in second or even last. The message here is to do your best and recognize when someone else's best exceeds yours.

There are situations in your life when you are excellent. What do you deserve a gold medal in? What is your passion? Is it cooking a meal or changing a tire? Do you put your heart and soul into what you are doing and try to do your best? Do you possibly deserve praise and recognition for the relationships in your life? Maybe you are the world's best friend! Notice I use the word best. Your best is good enough and sufficient in all areas. Strive to be good enough, and then, if you have a desire to go further, do so with intensity and passion.

Who can honestly say, *I only give a portion of what I have to offer?* This might be the case, but for the most part, if you are on the path to self-actualization, self-awareness and balance in your life, if your intentions are good and honest, the result will always be honorable. If you are not giving of yourself lovingly and honestly, today is the day to examine your life and make a concerted effort to put your best foot forward. You are amazing. Peace of mind that you are at your best trumps the need to win, at all costs, every time.

December 20

Affirmation: Today when I need a break, I will take a break.

"Rest" and "relaxation" are not dirty words. If your goal is to be your best in body, mind, and spirit, think rationally and treat others with dignity and respect. Then take time out of your busy day to step back when you are feeling stressed, tired, or overwhelmed. You don't always have to plow forward. Not only will you benefit, but the people around you will, as well. It is vital to take yourself out of the mix every now and then. You are indispensable in certain areas of your life, and you are also dispensable (contrary to popular belief) in others. There is always someone else available to help you when you are overloaded. If there isn't anyone to stand in for you, than this is an area of concern, one that needs to be addressed. And so for today, instead of pushing yourself beyond your limits, becoming angry or frustrated, and shutting down altogether, take a moment to acknowledge the need for a break, a nap, or a walk.

December 21

Affirmation: Today I will love my family members who encourage and challenge me.

This time of year I think of the love I have for my family and friends. The holidays are beginning for most of us and a new year is quickly approaching. It is not easy, as you are likely well aware, to foster a relationship of togetherness, humor, and mutual admiration with your family of origin. It is difficult to recreate, maintain, or perhaps establish for the first time a loving family bond. Some give up on family members for various reasons. Perhaps your parents are no longer in your life, or they have passed on. Perhaps a sister or a brother is creating strife, and you are called on to learn assertiveness and patience. Perhaps a brother-in-law or an uncle pushes your buttons, and you must practice restraint. The season of family is upon us, and it is the time to reconnect and show our love to the people in our lives who have given life—our lives. Thank the people in your life who bring hardship and difficulty. They are in your life for a reason.

December 22

Affirmation: I will remain calm and peaceful today.

When is the best time to take a daily *time out* for you? The suggestion of an adult *time out* is a gift I am giving you today. If you are twenty-five years old, take twenty-five minutes to yourself each day. If you are sixty years old, you get an hour to yourself!

Why is it so important to, to carve a calm and serene moment, free of distraction and excess noise, out of your day? Because it is good for your body, mind and spirit. Time to meditate is nourishment for the soul. A peaceful and quiet setting has restorative properties. *Alone time* can be calming, soothing and relaxing. Silence can bring peace to our day; allowing us to be a nicer person to be around. Meditation and prayer is the antidote for chaos and confusion.

There is no one size fits all way to mediate. There is no "mumbo jumbo" way to pray. Simply take time to sit quietly, where there are no distractions, close your eyes and concentrate on your breathing. When you concentrate on slowing your breathing; visualize a calm and peaceful place. Perhaps your vision is a waterfall or a beach on a summer's day. Let the thoughts of the day go. Be still. When you are ready, open your eyes and feel renewed and rejuvenated. Take a class or get a meditation tape that has instructions and peaceful music. You can download guided meditations on you computer or cell phone.

Ironically, people tell me that they are too busy to take time for themselves. This message is exactly what they need to hear! The holidays are a perfect time to reflect and slow down. Give the gift of peace and quiet to yourself, even if just for today.

December 23

Affirmation: Today I will work on my connections with my partner, my family, and my friends.

Day-to-day interaction is important when staying connected to the people we love and care about in our lives. Being honest, being dependable, and being supportive are just a few ways that nurture healthy relationships between individuals, families, and communities. Shared goals and dreams are conducive to healthy partnerships. If two people are very different, it is important to recognize the differences and learn and grow from being with that person. A parent/child relationship flourishes when the parent does not insist his or her child conform to the parent's patterns of behavior and expectations.

In the work environment, there are many different personalities, skill sets, and qualities that enhance productivity. Be aware that if someone is different from you it is natural and normal to disagree. We butt heads with others from time to time; this is how productivity is achieved. If everyone were the same, there would be no need for a diverse workforce. Getting along and cooperating with the people in our lives are the bedrock of being balanced and connected. Our health, happiness, and wellness depend on it.

December 24

Affirmation: Today I will keep it simple. I want to enjoy life.

If you want something from someone or have a question, all you have to do is ask. If you are thinking of someone and wondering how that person is, pick up the phone and call him or her. If you are feeling misunderstood, take the time to explain yourself so that others understand the full meaning of what it is that you are trying to get across. When feeling out of sorts, let others know how much you appreciate them, and ask them how you can help them. Why? Reaching out to others, in an assertive manner, is what being balanced and connected is all about. It is simply caring about and being respectful to yourself and others.

Being kind and loving to other people comes back to us tenfold. Many of us know the concept of karma but may not recognize the power it has over us. Karma refers to the principle of intention of an individual's words, actions, or deeds. Karma is also the concept of the Golden Rule. "Do unto others as you would have them do unto you." Good intentions and good deeds contribute to good karma and future happiness, while bad intentions and bad deeds contribute to bad karma and future suffering. Keep it simple, and try not to get bogged down and complicate your life. Enjoy the holidays, your friends and your family simply.

December 25

Affirmation: I wish love, peace, and kindness to all.

The most important thing we can do to obtain peace in our lives is to love our family. World peace starts with peace at home. For some, or perhaps most, peace is elusive. Perhaps you are able to find peaceful moments throughout the day. During very stressful periods in our life we might go for long stretches of time living with chaos. To obtain and sustain longer-lasting stretches of peace in body, mind, and spirit, we must think about what we are doing currently that prevents or destroys our contented state of being. Then gather the tools and support needed to ensure a more peaceful existence and a more loving and caring environment.

Keep the holiday spirit alive throughout the year. When you come home from work, de-stress and let the cares of the day go. Be more loving. Be helpful and playful with your family. Take a walk; eat good, healthy food; and take time to be still.

December 26

Affirmation: Self-respect comes from the ability to accept responsibility for your own life.

Do you like yourself? Really? Oftentimes people question whether they love themselves or even like who they are and what they stand for. Ask yourself, "Would I want to spend the day with myself?" Self-esteem and self-respect are concepts hard to come by for many. Many people struggle with the choices they make, the lives they lead, the actions they take, and the people they are. If we are not happy with ourselves, we blame others for our shortcomings. We do not take responsibility for our negative actions either because we know we're wrong and don't want to admit it, or we are in denial of our culpability.

Take the time at this year's end to think about what you like about yourself and what needs improvement. Focus on how you really feel about yourself. When you look in the mirror, are you content with your circumstances—your career, surroundings, and relationships? Where is there room for improvement? Are you happy with the way you talk to other people and how you handle your emotions? Are you kind? We can all make adjustments; I try on a daily basis! We all have room for improvement. I never believe anyone who tells me he or she is perfectly fine and absolutely nothing is out of balance in his or her life. If this is the case, I want what that person is having.

December 27

Affirmation: I am in a good place. I have let go of animosity, hatred, and jealousy.

If you find yourself in a negative space, animosity, hatred, or jealousy might be lurking. Animosity is hatred. If you're embarrassed, let down, or cheated by a friend, your friendship could turn into animosity, which is painful and nonproductive.

We can be the flowers and the trees and still be jealous of the sun and the sky. Religions and faith-based communities throughout the world teach tolerance, unity, peace, and nonviolence. Love has the power to open our hearts to happiness and turn our hearts and minds away from hatred and jealousy. Jealousy is trying and hurtful to others but is also destructive to us.

Life is full of choices and opportunities. Surround yourself with positive and meaningful people, not the types of people who constantly put you down and want what you have. Run from negative and toxic people if you must. Be true to yourself, and be well.

December 28

Affirmation: I look to my source of strength and energy to fill me with grace.

When we give of our hearts and minds to another person, with joy and kindness in our hearts, it is then that we are in a state of grace. We don't pretend we are people we're not. We are not always the people who say yes when we don't want to, or the people who always say no. We are true to our words and our promises. When we are in a state of grace, we are loyal, trusting, and reliable. Everyone benefits when we are authentic in what we say and do, when we are honest and kind. Not only are these healthy and positive virtues but they also carry with them divine qualities.

At this most holy time of year, let us take a moment to examine our hearts and minds and see what we can do better in our lives and in our relationships with others. Open up your heart and mind to become more aware and tolerant of other people's ways, cultures, and circumstances that are different from yours. It is easy to be there for other people who are like you, but it is not so easy to be open to others who are different. It is exactly when we open ourselves up to people who are seemingly different that we truly grow and our minds and hearts expand exponentially. The next time you meet a stranger, be open to the possibility of love. These actions bring grace to our lives.

December 29

Affirmation: Today I will try my hardest.

At times I am guilty of beginning my day in a cranky mood. I get out of bed, and, before doing anything else, I make myself a cup of coffee. I think to myself that I can pray and meditate after my first cup. I think to myself that I am beginning my day off on the right foot. Within a few moments, I realize that the coffee is kicking in and I begin to feel the effects of the caffeine. So much for meditating! On the days I postpone the coffee and pray and meditate first thing upon waking, I find that my day progresses much smoother and I am able to be in control of my thoughts and emotions in a more loving and self-affirming way.

Why am I confessing that I do not take my own advice every day of the year? I want you to know that it is not easy to navigate life in a calm and relaxed manner. It is as hard for me as it might be for you to live a self-assured, self-actualizing existence.

What I do know for sure—and I would like to thank you for indulging me—is that the words and actions of each one of us can be attempted only one day at a time. Each morning we are given new opportunities to start the day with good intentions in mind. Then by midday perhaps we find ourselves falling back into old, familiar patterns. What can we do when our days didn't go exactly as we planned? Recognize what is going wrong, what our triggers are, and try again tomorrow and the next day and the next.

It's often said that old habits die hard. New habits are not formed overnight. After much trial and error, after reading the words in this book carefully, thoughtfully, and with contemplative reflection, you might just find that you have changed in an area of your life, possibly for the better. This is a book that can be read anytime, anywhere. Perhaps a thought or suggestion bears repeating. By all means go over it again and again until you feel good about what it is you are now incorporating into your daily life. We are on this journey together.

December 30

Affirmation: This is not the end. It's a new beginning.

From an early age we are conditioned to think in a linear fashion, where there is a beginning, middle, and end. Things start, they happen, and they end. Sometimes we want something to end, other times we resist, and yet other times we may have a mixed reaction.

When something ends there exists a void that is created by the ending of one thing and the beginning of something else. A key to moving forward is being aware, being open, and being receptive to who or how or what may be on the horizon. More important is to stay where you are in the moment and enjoy the ride. Experience the grandeur of the heights and the lows, as well. It is enough to trust that something new and different will come along. Don't curse your current situation or fear the next.

There is a wonderful, mystical, magical continuity of experience and awareness, where endings become new beginnings. The more you trust that when one thing ends, another begins, you are able to relax and let the power of faith, hope, and love happen through the struggle.

December 31

Affirmation: On this year's end I will call to mind that I am experienced and wise, and I think consciously and clearly.

To know that you are experienced doesn't mean you have to be in the golden years of your life. The same thing goes for being wise. Regardless of your age, you have experience in some area of your life. Little children and young adults are not often looked to for their expertise, but they do have a lot to say, a lot of knowledge, and insight. Everyone's opinion matters. The definition of *wise* is to be informed. Anyone at any age can certainly be informed regarding something! Don't underestimate how wise you truly are. Everyone is different. Everyone is unique, and everyone has different abilities, likes and dislikes, and interests.

I was the youngest of five children. When I was a little girl, no one took me seriously or asked for my opinion. At an early age, I set a goal for myself. I would become knowledgeable in something —anything. I would be able to talk with people and feel comfortable knowing that, not only did I know what I was talking about, but I, in fact, had something to contribute to the conversation. To this day, I am told that I talk to people, regardless of who they are, with ease. Mission accomplished.

May there be peace on earth for everyone.

Epilogue

God 101

The principal object of belief or faith around the world, the idea of God, as commonly described by theologians, includes:

1. Omniscience (infinite knowledge)
2. Omnipotence (unlimited power)
3. Omnipresence (present everywhere, perfect goodness)
4. Omnibenevolence (eternal and necessary existence and divine simplicity)

{God} = monotheism (one); {g}od = henotheism (many).

God is the creator and sustainer of the universe, as described in *theism,* as opposed to *deism*, which describes God as creator of the universe but not the sustainer of the planet. The belief in the oneness of God is *monotheism. Pantheism* is the belief that God is the universe. *Panentheism* believes that everything is "all-in-God." *Atheism* is the belief that God purportedly does not exist, while *agnosticism* deems that the existence of a God is unknowable or unknown. This is heavy stuff!

God is described by some as immaterial (incorporeal). To some believers, God is the source of morality and virtue, all that is good. To others, God is a personal source of being. Philosophers throughout time have disputed and continue to dispute the existence of God. What I know for certain is what I teach the children. God is in the word *g(o)od*, and evil is in the word *(d)evil.*

Acknowledgements

To my professional mentor, Nina Bravman, Ed.S., director of the Center for Human Potential, Denville, New Jersey, for teaching me absolutely everything I know about being a psychotherapist in private practice. To Dr. Charlie McNeil, LMFT; Beverly Carboy, educator (ret); and Marie Grace O'Brien for their tremendous help editing my thoughts and words. To Jill Rodda, Personal Yoga Training, for keeping me balanced and connected. To my research assistant on *Always Balanced and Connected*, Devin O'Brien, for the countless hours of help with everything beginning with the inception of this book. Devin is a true gentleman and a scholar. To my friends and mentors JoAnn Moffitt, LCSW, of Marysville Washington School District, and Frank Busichio, LCSW, WA State Department of Corrections (ret.). To my colleagues in Sussex County, New Jersey, for the past twenty-five years: Faith A. Ullman, Esq.; Dr. Seth Ersner-Hershfeld; Nelson L. Hadler, LCSW, LCADC, Treatment Dynamics of Summit; Tulasi Jordan, LCSW; Diane Quatrone Carroll, LCSW; Marybeth Colville Ferrie, Pat Kibildis, MSW; Donna Fell/ Indie Books; George F. Dyer, DMD, Drs. Jeffrey S. Panicucci, DMD; and Christopher G. Quimette, DMD; Dr. Michele Takacs; Geri Daugherty; Pierce Skinner, Psy.D; Deborah Templeton, APNC, Lac; Paul Littman, MD; Frank Kane, MD, and Robert Pampin, DO; Scott J. Ruvo, DDS and Nancy Ruvo, educator (ret); Brian Trautz, DC, CH, CI; Al Vonderahe; Marshall Okin, Samantha LeValley; Ryan Moffitt; Garret LaFranco; Scott Klinger and Jackie George Klinger; Chuck and Mary Jo Mathias, our friends at Sussex County Arts and Heritage Council and Diane Taylor and Kelly Bonventre of Pass-It-Along. To my talented research assistants, Ellen Tremiti, writer, film/media specialist and Alexandra McDonald, PhD (candidate), career counselor, CUNY. To Maryann McFadden, writer; Dawn Hamilton, writer; Irene Breznak, writer; Philip Takas-Senske, Esq.; Brett Becker, Esq.; Anna Becker, RNP; Frank Kane, Jr., USMC; Nicholas Eliades, Esq.; Ginny Eliades; Paris Eliades, Esq.; David Bloemer; the Dyrsten family; the Tiene family. To my friends in faith, Donna Centrelli and Arlene Michel Rich, spiritual counselors and Marianne O'Brien Walsh. To my Ramapo family; Kelly Pampin, BSW, Ramapo College of New Jersey; Kim Blazier Rogalsky, RCNJ; Rebecca Bloom Lupo, RCNJ; Craig Kalucki, RCNJ; Charlotte Cort, RCNJ; Lori Genung, BSW, RCNJ. To Christina Knips Jelly, business/educator; Trevor O'Brien, Harvard University and Leah Marinello O'Brien, child and family care specialist; Meghan Johnson, music educator/SUNY; Emily Marquez, Penn State University; Leslie Meskin, LCSW; Eryn Greenstein, behavioral health specialist; Jennifer Wolgast, Nutritionist; Danny Scialla, Musician/Artist; Lee Suckno, MD; Dory Rachel, RMT; Carole Schildkamp DeBonte, RD; Ashley Iannone, student/ Boston University; Michael J. Foley, educator; Michael Patrick Foley; Evan T. Jelly, MSc, biotechnology; Alexander D. Jelly, CGBP; Nora M. Jelly, Nutrition, UNCG; Julie Randazzo, student/ Universite Francois-Rabelais; Glennis Randazzo, RN, Charleston, SC School District; Andrea Ames; Glenna Butler, social worker (ret.); Marian Van Gorder, MSW, Florida State University; Jen Valdelon Turetsky, RNP, Memorial Sloan-Kettering Cancer Center, NYC; Thomas Joseph Davis, educator, DOD, Germany; Karen Carney, educator (ret); Melanie Davis, PhD, CSE; Bernard Garforth; and Joseph Garforth, Bradford-on-Avon, England, UK and George Garforth, Sheffield, England, UK; Hilde de Vos, Clinical and Health Psychology, Bruge, Belgium; Fabien Charles; Michael May; David Hill, student/ UNCG; Astrid le Clerc, DO and Nicolas Svetchine, Journalist, Paris, France; Lea Jean-Jean, Psychology, Toulouse, France; Cynthia Wright Kolsen; Wanda Blake, artist/mentor; Peggy Fitzpatrick, PC, Parenting Resources; Nancy Mueller-Davis; Lt. Colonel Gary Trageser, USAF (ret); Delaney Xenakis; Rachel Paulson, HOW Global; Kaelyn Siverski; Patrice Lenowitz, Children's Justice Campaign; Cherese Rambaldi and Mira Rambaldi of the Nurtured Parent; Amy Hoff and friends at the West Tisbury Free Public Library, Martha's Vineyard, Massachusetts; Terry Real, LICSW, and Lisa Sullivan, Relational Life Institute. A very special acknowledgement to the artful genius of Vineyard Colors of Martha's Vineyard, MA. To Adriane Pontecorvo, and Staci Kern who have been kind, helpful and amazing throughout the entire publication process; Shelby Owen and Karol Canada, marketing and publicity team at Balboa Press, a Division of Hay House Publishing; and Dana G. Cohen, MD.

To my brothers and sisters, aunts, uncles, cousins, nieces, nephews, in-laws, out-laws, and their families, thank you for keeping me balanced and connected. To the educators, physicians, psychiatrists, neurologists, nutritionists, primary care physicians, pediatricians, attorneys, judges, victims' rights advocates, DCPP/DYFS/CPS workers, law enforcement, bereavement specialists, clergy, caregivers, coaches, guidance counselors, and friends of my patients and their families, too many to name, who have touched my heart and spirit. Collectively, you have made me stronger and have given me courage and the insight that I will never walk alone. It is my intention that you will someday know how *I'm* feeling!

Be well,

Maggie

Contributors

Dana Cohen, MD, is renowned by her peers and beloved by patients for her refined practice of Integrative Medicine. In practice for over fifteen years, she trained under the late Dr. Robert Atkins, author of the iconic *Dr. Atkins' New Diet Revolution*, and Dr. Ronald L. Hoffman, a pioneer of integrative medicine and founder of the Hoffman Center in New York City. She earned her MD from St. George's University School of Medicine and completed a three-year internal medicine residency at Albany Medical Center. Dr. Cohen was certified by the American Board of Internal Medicine in 1998 and was recently appointed to the Board of Directors of the American College for the Advancement of Medicine (ACAM), the leading voice of Integrative Medicine for more than 1,500 MD, DO, ND, and master-level health-care providers, where she is also program director of their biyearly symposiums.

Dr. Charlie McNeil, LMFT, is in private practice as a Psychotherapist and Marriage and Family Therapist (licensed since 1983). He is a Clinical Fellow in AAMFT, an ordained United Methodist minister (retired), and an Adjunct Professor at Drew University. He and his wife, Jane McKeever, live in Allamuchy, New Jersey.

Jill Rodda, MS, is a certified personal trainer (American Council on Education) and a personal yoga instructor and wellness coach since 2008. She has an MS in Business Management. Jill is a member of IDEA Fitness. She resides with her family in Lake Mohawk, New Jersey.

About the Author

Maggie Davis-Jelly, LCSW, is in private practice as a Licensed Clinical Social Worker in the New York/New Jersey metro area. Maggie graduated from Ramapo College of New Jersey in 1985. A Graduate School of Social Work student at NYU, she left to raise her family and continued on to graduate from Rutgers University, NJ/MSW/LCSW program, in 1991. Maggie started "Art by Me: Photography and Art for Non-Profits" in 1999. Maggie is a past board member of Family Promise of Sussex County, where she has continued to volunteer for the past twenty years. Maggie volunteers for H.O.W. Global, Inc., and Pass-it-Along, Inc. Maggie is an advocate for victims of domestic violence and volunteers for the Nurtured Parent and the Children's Justice Campaign, both nonprofit organizations that raise awareness by speaking out against and lending support to empower survivors of domestic violence. Maggie has been a student of martial arts at East West Karate Academy, Sussex County, New Jersey, beginning in 1997.

Maggie lives with her husband, Bill. Together they have grown children: Evan Thomas Jelly of Boston, Massachusetts; Alexander Davis Jelly; Christina Marie Knips Jelly of Andover, New Jersey; and Nora Margaret Jelly of Greensboro, NC. The Jelly family resides in Sussex County, New Jersey, and West Tisbury, Massachusetts.

Approximately twenty-six million Americans suffer from a mental disorder, and twenty million suffer from a mood disorder, including depression and bipolar disorder. Of that twenty million, fifteen million Americans suffer from major depression that does not easily go away and requires treatment by a doctor and/or a mental health professional. The good news is there is treatment. Getting help is the hardest step, but it is the first step to feeling better and the only step oftentimes to living a balanced lifestyle. Are you someone who feels helpless and hopeless? Do you have anxiety and say things like "I'm stressed out" or "I don't have the time?" Are you overweight or underweight and unhealthy? Do you suffer from clinical depression, anxiety, or addiction? Please, consider taking a moment to get real and get help! Help is available. Talk to a physician, clergyperson, social worker, nurse, teacher, family member, or friend who can recommend someone. By all means, get counsel, get better, and get help.

Help!

Need help?

In the United States, call 800-273-8255 (National Suicide Prevention Lifeline)

National Domestic Violence Hotline: 800-799-7233 or TTY 800-787-3224

NAMI.org (National Association on Mental Illness)

NEDA.org (National Eating Disorders Association)

www.eatingdisordersanonymous.org

SAMHSA.gov (Substance Abuse and Mental Health Service Administration)

Childhelp National Child Abuse Hotline: 800-4-A-CHILD (800-422-4453)

Depression and Bipolar Support Alliance: 800-826-3632

Mental Health America (for a referral to a specific mental health service or support program in your community): 800-969-NMHA (6642)

National Alliance on Mental Illness (provides support, information, and referrals): 800-950-NAMI (6264)

National Association of Anorexia Nervosa and Associated Disorders: 847-831-3438

National Center for Posttraumatic Stress Disorder: 802-296-6300

National Center for Victims of Crime (multilingual service available): 800-FYI-CALL (394-2255)

National Drug and Alcohol Treatment Hotline (treatment referrals): 800-662-HELP (4357)

National Domestic Violence Hotline: 800-799-SAFE (7233)

National Eating Disorders Association Information and Referral Helpline (support services, help, and guidance to people struggling with eating disorders, their loved ones, and families): 800-931-2237

National Runaway Switchboard: 800-RUNAWAY (800-786-2929)

National Sexual Assault Hotline: 800-656-HOPE (4673)

National Suicide Prevention Hotline: 800-273-TALK (8255)

Postpartum Support International: 800-994-4PPD (4773)

PPD Hope: 877-PPD-HOPE (877-773-4673)

PPD Moms: 800-PPD-MOMS (800-773-6667)

CDC National AIDS Clearinghouse (information and publication orders): 800-458-5231; TTY 800-243-1098; international 301-562-1098, TTY international 301-588-1586 (English and Spanish)

Www.projectinform.org (HIV/AIDS Hotlines and Project Inform)

National Hotlines. CDC National AIDS Hotline: 800-CDC-INFO (800-232-4636) or TTY 1-888-232-6348 (24/7) English and Spanish.

800-DONTCUT (800-366-8288)

For any emergency in the United States, call 911.

In the United Kingdom, call 999
In the European Union, call 112

On some networks a GSM phone without a SIM card may be used to make emergency calls. Most GSM phones accept a larger list of emergency numbers without a SIM card, such as 112, 911, 118, 119, 000, 110, 08, and 999. However, some GSM networks will not accept emergency calls from phones without a SIM card, or even require a SIM card that has credit.

If the affirmations in this book are working for you and you're seeing things in a different light, please let me know. I welcome feedback. To contact Maggie Davis-Jelly, LCSW, for conferences, speaking engagements or fundraising for non-profits go to www.alwaysbalancedandconnected.com or www.maggiedavisjelly.com

References

Engelbreit, Mary/ www.goodreads.com/.../94599

Sagan, Carl/ en.wikipedia.org/.../
Relationship_between_religion_and_scien…

Twain, Mark/www.goodreads.
com/.../505050-the-two-most-important-days...

Cover Photo: Vineyard Colors, Martha's Vineyard, MA

Author Photograph on Back Cover:
Garrett LaFranco, Sparta, NJ

Made in the USA
Middletown, DE
12 July 2016